THE BOOK OF
DISCOVERIES

THIS IS A WELBECK CHILDREN'S BOOK

Published in 2021 by Welbeck Children's Books
An imprint of Welbeck Children's Limited, part of
Welbeck Publishing Group
20 Mortimer Street London W1T 3JW

Produced under licence for SCMG Enterprises Ltd.
Science Museum® SCMG
Every purchase supports the museum.
www.sciencemuseum.org.uk

A CIP catalogue record for this book is available from the
British Library.

ISBN: 978-1-78312-594-4

Printed in China

10 9 8 7 6 5 4 3 2 1

Commissioning Editor: Bryony Davies
Managing Art Editor: Matt Drew
Designer: Claire Clewley
Production: Melanie Robertson

Published in association with the

SCIENCE MUSEUM

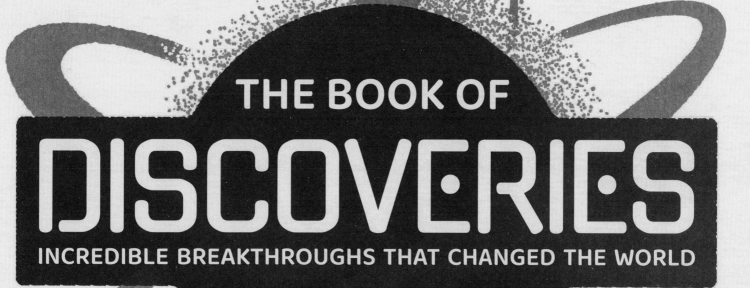

THE BOOK OF
DISCOVERIES
INCREDIBLE BREAKTHROUGHS THAT CHANGED THE WORLD

WRITTEN BY TIM COOKE

ILLUSTRATED BY DREW BARDANA

WELBECK

Contents

1

Making Things Move

Forces

2

Building Blocks of Life

Biology

3

Staying Healthy

Medicine

Aerodynamics

Dinosaurs

Introduction

What is a discovery? It's when you observe, learn or explain something for the first time – but not just anything. It's not like learning the French word for 'breakfast' or where the nearest supermarket is. A discovery isn't learning something that *you* didn't know. It's learning something that *no one* knew but that was always there, waiting to be found out.

Take an apple falling off a tree. Everyone knows that it falls to the ground. But until the 1660s, no one knew why. That's when the English scientist Isaac Newton suggested that

a force was pulling the apple to the ground, and he named the force gravity. Newton then used maths to show that this gravity applied to everything, everywhere.

Like many other discoveries, the idea didn't come out of the blue as a 'ta-da!' moment, and Newton wasn't the first person to ever wonder about the topic. Other scientists such as Galileo Galilei had already explored ideas about falling objects, and Newton himself was inspired by his own work on calculus – a mathematical way to study objects in motion. The apple might have helped Newton, but his 'breakthrough' was in fact one of a series of steps, as scientists built on earlier insights.

Algebra

Radioactivity

It Takes Dedication

Newton's apple is one of the most famous stories of scientific discovery, but there are many others, each made by all sorts of different people. It might be easy to assume that only extraordinary scientists with years of research and training behind them can make important discoveries, but that's simply not true. Many discoveries were based on careful observation and deduction, and were made by more ordinary people, just like you (although of course, we're not saying you won't turn out to be a genius!).

Explaining the World Around Us

Some discoveries happened so long ago that no one knows who made them. Who was the first human to discover that fire burned? Or that some foods taste better cooked than raw? Perhaps one of our early ancestors tried eating an animal that had been partly burned in a wildfire and liked the taste. Fast-forwarding much later in history, who discovered that storing avocados with bananas helps the avocados ripen?

All these phenomena were discovered at different times – but of course some were more important than others. Not only did these discoveries explain many phenomena in the world around us, but the increased understanding they brought enabled advances in technology that have benefited us all.

Making Things Move

Forces

Everything in the universe is in motion: planets orbit the Sun, apples fall to the ground, magnets pull each other together or push each other apart and invisible waves move through the air. Since early history, thinkers have tried to understand the forces that cause different kinds of motion and other phenomena. Their discoveries have led to a remarkable understanding of the shape of the universe and the forces that affect our lives, from the nature of magnetism and electricity to how light travels – and how to throw a stick so that it comes back!

Magnetism

According to legend, the first magnet was discovered about 4,000 years ago when a shepherd in ancient Greece found that the iron nails in his shoes and crook stuck to a stone in the ground. The shepherd's name was Magnes so it didn't take much imagination to call the stone magnetite – from which comes our word 'magnetism'.

Whether or not this story is true, the ancient Greeks certainly knew about magnets. Greek writer Thales of Miletus thought that magnetic objects had souls because they could move iron.
In China, too, people saw pieces of magnetite, often called lodestones, or 'stones that lead', as

mystical. People realized that not only did the stones attract iron, but that pieces of magnetite would, without being touched, arrange themselves so they pointed north and south.
The Earth has its own magnetic field, and, like any magnetized object, it has a north and a south pole. These poles are what the magnetized pieces of magnetite (try saying that in a hurry) were lining up with. The Chinese originally used pieces of lodestone as pointers in fortune-telling, making them into shapes such as fish, turtles and spoons.

Nifty Navigation
It isn't known exactly when, but possibly around the 10th century, and certainly by the 12th century, both Chinese navigators and Viking sailors from

Scandinavia were using magnetized needles to find their way at sea. The needle would float on a piece of straw in a bowl of water, and would always turn to point north/south. Once sailors knew which way was north, they could work out other directions, too.

Out on the Open Ocean

Now sailors did not have to rely on the Sun, the stars or landmarks to navigate. In the 15th century, open ocean sailing really took off – and so did the compass. Ships could sail for days, weeks or months out of sight of land, using the compass to navigate. When Portuguese explorer Ferdinand Magellan set off on a voyage around the world in 1519, he took spare compass needles with him, just in case.

Magnetic North

In the late 1500s, English physician William Gilbert constructed a model of Earth to study why a compass points north. He decided that the planet had an iron core that created a huge magnetic field over the planet. Scientists later realized that the pole of this magnetic field – 'magnetic north' – did not quite line up with the geographical north pole, the northernmost point on the planet, which we call the 'North Pole'. Magnetic north also moves around. So it was quite an achievement for James Ross, a British naval officer, to find it in 1831. He was disappointed to find only ice, rather than a big magnetic rock.

Gravity

The story of how Isaac Newton discovered gravity is famous: an apple fell from a tree as he sat beneath it. Perhaps the apple hit his head. Whatever the truth – some people say the tale is not true – what's important is that lots of people had seen things fall to the ground before, but Newton set out to discover why.

This was not Newton's first discovery. Not long after graduating from university in 1665, he had made breakthroughs in maths, such as discovering calculus, which is a way of studying things that constantly change.

Now Newton began to wonder about why an apple always fell towards the ground, and not up or to either side. Other people had noticed the effects of gravity, of course. In Italy, Galileo Galilei had studied the speed of falling objects, for example. But no one had explained *why* things fell.

Invisible Force

Newton had read the works of Galileo, and also of the French thinker René Descartes, who argued

Aha... gravity!

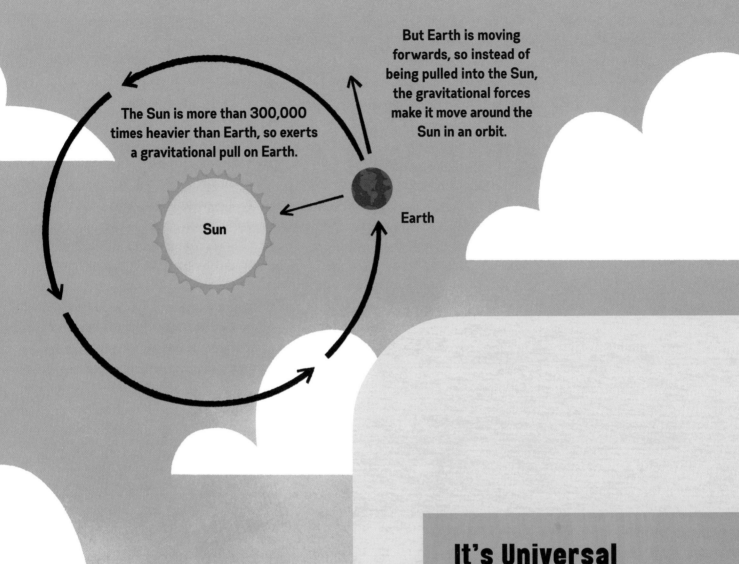

The Sun is more than 300,000 times heavier than Earth, so exerts a gravitational pull on Earth.

But Earth is moving forwards, so instead of being pulled into the Sun, the gravitational forces make it move around the Sun in an orbit.

Sun

Earth

that all natural phenomena resulted from an interaction between tiny particles that made up all matter.

Using Descartes' idea, Newton suggested that every object in the universe exerts a force of attraction on every other object. That force, gravity, explains why the apple fell – and also why the planets orbit the Sun. Earth's gravity is many times greater than that of an apple, so Earth pulls the apple towards the ground. The Sun is so much bigger than Earth that, although it is far away, its gravity holds Earth in its orbit.

Newton's discovery of universal gravitation was a huge scientific advance, and his theory is still used.

It's Universal

Decades after he discovered gravity, in 1687, Newton published the law of universal gravitation. This mathematical formula explained how gravity shaped the whole universe, from the very small to the very large. The law says that every particle attracts other particles with a force that is directly proportional to the product of their masses and inversely proportional to the square of the distance between their centres. In other words, the strength of gravity depends on the size of the objects compared to each other and their distance from one another.

Laws of Motion

If you put a ball on a flat surface, it stays there. If someone kicks it, it travels until it hits something or slows down and stops. If it hits another ball, they both bounce off each other at opposite angles. Those things seem pretty ordinary – but the same laws that cover a rolling ball also explain how horses run and aeroplanes fly, and why the planets orbit the Sun. Discovering these laws was a huge step forward for, well, understanding the world around us.

We already know Isaac Newton was one smart cookie (see pages 12-13). He was one of the stars of the Scientific Revolution, a period during the 16th and 17th centuries when scientists tried using observation to work out the natural laws (or rules) that shaped the universe.

Going Through the Motions

Along with all his other interests, Newton wanted to know more about motion. But he was not the only one: the Italian astronomer Galileo Galilei had recently suggested that an object that is still or moving will remain in that state until an external force, or 'push', acts on it.

Newton developed Galileo's idea, and added observations of his own to come up with three laws or rules:

1. An object will remain still, or a moving object won't change speed or direction, unless an external force acts upon it.

According to this law, a ball rolls in a straight line until it is knocked in a different direction or until friction (an external force) slows it down.

2. The bigger the force that moves an object, the further and faster it will move.

A powerful jet engine creates enough force to push a large aeroplane quickly through the air. The bigger the force it creates, the faster the aeroplane flies.

3. For every action, such as a push, there is an equal and opposite reaction.

A horse pushes its hooves against the ground, which pushes back, so the horse moves forwards.

So that's it. The mechanics of virtually everything explained in just a few lines. That's pretty impressive.

Plenty of Laws

We've used one example to explain each law of motion, but in reality, all Newton's laws apply to anything that moves. Unless you switch the engine on, a plane will remain still (law 1). The bigger the force of a jet engine, the faster a plane moves (law 2). The jet engine makes the plane move because it pushes a jet of exhaust out of the back. When it is pushed by this exhaust jet, the air pushes back (law 3), making the plane move forwards. It was understanding the laws of motion that allowed engineers to invent and develop the jet engine, enabling large aeroplanes to take to the skies.

Law 1

Law 2

Law 3

Electricity

When inventors made electrical devices in the late 1800s, their contemporaries hailed a modern Age of Electricity. In fact, electricity had been known about for many centuries. After all, people in the past had been struck by lightning, which is a form of electricity, or stung by electric eels.

Electricity is a kind of energy created by tiny, negatively charged particles called electrons. Static electricity was discovered first. The ancient Greeks wrote about it – and about getting electric shocks from fish.

Getting Static

When certain objects are rubbed together, the electrons inside their atoms can be transferred from one object to another. Electrons are negatively charged, so if lots of them move to one object, it will become negatively charged. The other object, which has lost electrons, will be positively charged. Two items that have the same charge repel each other. If they have different charges, or if one is charged and one is not charged, they will attract each other – like the man and the objects on the plate in the demonstration below.

In the 1500s, an Elizabethan scientist named William Gilbert created a static electrical charge by

rubbing a hard orange material called amber, which the Greeks had also used. The Greek name for amber was elektron, so the force came to be known as electricity. Two hundred years later, people in Georgian England used machines to create static electricity for entertainment.

Going Electric

Electricity became the subject of intense research. In 1800, an Italian nobleman named Alessandro Volta made the first battery, which produced a current that flowed around a conductor, such as a wire. In the early 1800s, Michael Faraday built an electric motor that could drive machines, and Georg Ohm figured out how an electrical circuit actually worked. Centuries after people first discovered electricity, the Age of Electricity was about to begin.

Franklin's Kite

In 1752 Benjamin Franklin carried out one of the most famous – and dangerous – experiments in history. He flew a kite during a thunderstorm on the end of a long, damp string. The kite gathered electricity from the air and carried it to a metal key Franklin tied near the bottom of the string. When Franklin put his hand next to the key, he got an electric shock – which left him overjoyed. He had shown that, during storms, the air was full of electricity, which is what creates lightning. (If an actual lightning bolt had struck the kite, however, the charge would have been so powerful that Franklin would probably have died.)

And now to demonstrate the amazing power of static electricity!

Electromagnetism

After Alessandro Volta invented the first electric battery in 1800, scientists could create a stable electrical current for the first time. That sparked a rush of scientific investigation ('Sparked'. Electricity. Get it?) – and led to the discovery of electromagnetism.

Studious Scientists

These investigations were carried out by scientists such as Danish pharmacist Hans Christian Ørsted, who was intrigued by the suggestion that electricity and magnetism were related. He, like many natural philosophers (what we would now call scientists) at the time, was investigating whether all the physical forces were connected.

In 1820, Ørsted passed an electric current through a wire, which moved the needle of a nearby magnetic compass. The current created a magnetic field around the wire.

This discovery allowed the French scientist André-Marie Ampère to go one step further and create an 'electromagnet' by passing a current through two parallel wires to attract them together or push them apart.

In a Spin

In 1821 the British scientist Michael Faraday tried applying an electric current to a metal rod that was dipped in a vessel of mercury with a magnet in its centre. The rod rapidly circled the magnet. This movement – called electromagnetic rotation – made it possible to turn electrical energy into mechanical energy.

Induction Deduction

A decade later, Faraday learned that a changing magnetic field causes electricity to flow in a circuit. He rotated copper wires rapidly around a magnet to induce a current, turning mechanical energy into electrical energy. Meanwhile, the U.S. physicist Joseph Henry was also working on this process – electromagnetic induction – discovering it for himself just a year later.

Faraday used electromagnetic induction to build the first electric motor. Today, it is still the principal idea behind all types of electric motor, along with the massive turbines and dynamos that generate electrical power for everyone to use.

No Need for Study

Faraday carried out many experiments to learn more about electromagnetism, and his discoveries have led to inventions you might use every day, such as a fridge or a car. He was a very skilled scientist and loved to experiment, but Faraday did not have a very broad education and maths was not his strong suit. It was actually the Scottish mathematician James Clerk Maxwell who came up with equations to explain the laws of electromagnetism in 1860, naming one after Faraday. So if you love to experiment but maths isn't your best subject, don't be put off! If Faraday could do it, so can you.

Nature of Light

Spare a thought for the British physicist Thomas Young. While everyone has heard of Isaac Newton (he's cropped up twice in this book already!), few people know about Young. That's not really fair, because in 1802 Young came up with an experiment to test the nature of light that showed that Newton was... gasp... WRONG!

Since ancient times, people have tried to understand light and how it behaves. Islamic scientists during the Middle Ages, for example, came to understand that light could be bent; that it spread out if it passed through a small opening and that it was possibly a type of wave.

Wave Goodbye...

So it was odd that in the early 1700s Newton decided that light travelled as a series of particles that were much smaller than particles of matter. Despite the evidence to the contrary, no one really challenged the mighty Newton for a hundred years, until along came Thomas Young.

Young shone a light onto a screen through two thin vertical slits, and he noted that the light was diffracted (bent) into a pattern of lighter and darker areas. This showed that light waves were spreading out from both slits and interfering with one another to create patterns. Not only did Young show that light travelled as a wave, but he also measured the wavelengths of the different colours of light.

And Wave Hello...

So that was settled... or was it? In the early 1900s another physicist suggested that light is not an ordinary wave but is made up of discrete, or separate, packets of energy. It sounded mad, but because that physicist was German scientist Albert Einstein, people took notice. Einstein suggested that light was made up of packets of energy, or 'quanta'. The brighter the light, the more quanta it has. Today, quanta are known as photons and scientists believe that light has the qualities of both a wave and a particle. So in a way everyone was right.

In the 1920s, Einstein's observation would give rise to a whole new branch of physics concerned with the behaviour of particles smaller than an atom: quantum mechanics.

A Famous Experiment

One of Newton's most famous experiments was to shine a beam of white light through a prism of glass. It bent into a rainbow of seven colours. Other people had observed the same thing in the past, but thought that the colours came from the glass. Newton used another prism to turn the colours back into white light – proving that the colours were in light, not in objects.

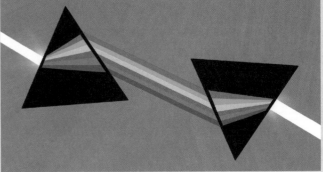

Conservation of Energy

In 1740, the French noblewoman Émilie du Châtelet decided to write a physics textbook for her 13-year-old son. In fact, she wrote one of the most important texts of the Scientific Revolution, which made her name as a leading scientist.

Du Châtelet was particularly interested in Isaac Newton, and in 1749 she translated his book *Principia* into French – and added some thoughts of her own. Among the subjects she was interested in was the nature of energy, which at the time was poorly understood. In the 1600s, the German Gottfried Wilhelm Leibniz had investigated the energy in mechanical systems, and he suggested that it was related to the mass and velocity of the parts of the system.

Now, Du Châtelet suggested that the energy contained in a closed system remained the same. It was merely transferred or changed into another form of energy. When a piece of coal is burned, for example, the chemical energy in the coal is converted into heat and light. Du Châtelet suggested that these different types of energy should be measured in the same units, because they are effectively the same thing.

Stimulating Partnership

Du Châtelet was outstanding at maths and physics, and her country estate had its own laboratory. She also had a romantic relationship with Voltaire, one of the most famous thinkers in Europe. When they both entered a competition to try to explain the nature of fire and light, Du Châtelet conducted her experiments secretly so Voltaire couldn't steal her findings.

Getting Warmer!

At the end of the 1700s, the nature of energy became clearer still. American-born British scientist Benjamin Thompson noticed that a drill bit became hot after drilling. He suggested that the heat was a form of energy created by the friction of the drill.

Between 1839 and 1850, the English physicist James Prescott Joule conducted a series of experiments and showed that heat and mechanical energy were closely connected. The unit of measurement, the joule, is named after him.

Falling from a Height

Du Châtelet investigated the conservation of energy with an experiment in which she dropped balls from different heights into soft clay. The size of the crater the balls created depended on their velocity, which was higher the further they had fallen. The amount of clay smashed aside measured the kinetic energy of the ball (the energy it has by moving), while the height from which it was dropped indicated its potential energy (the energy it has from being lifted up against gravity). Du Châtelet established that the kinetic energy of the ball was related to its potential energy.

Radio Waves

Imagine discovering something really, really important – and not realizing its significance. You're imagining the life of the German physicist Heinrich Hertz, who became the first man to understand the nature of radio waves in 1886. When he was asked what their practical application might be, he is supposed to have said, 'None at all.'

These are some of the answers Hertz could have given: the radio, the TV, the wireless telegraph, mobile phones, wifi, navigation, radio-controlled toys, drones and burglar alarms. But of course, many of these inventions were in the distant future.

Part of a Spectrum

In fact, Hertz didn't discover radio waves. That was the Scottish scientist James Clerk Maxwell, who in around 1864 predicted that light was a form of electromagnetic radiation or energy. Maxwell saw that there was a whole spectrum (range) of electromagnetic radiation, and that light was just the form that is visible to humans.

Radio waves are created by the reaction between electrical and magnetic fields. They are not visible,

It looks pretty useless to me.

but they are everywhere in the universe, travelling close to the speed of light.

Maxwell's calculations led Hertz to investigate how to create and detect radio waves. He set up a long copper wire between two large spheres of zinc and applied a high electrical charge to a gap he had left in the copper. That caused the wire to shake violently - generating radio waves that Hertz detected using a similar copper-wire receiver.

Broadcast News

Other scientists could see the potential of Hertz's discovery. In 1894, the Italian Guglielmo Marconi began experimenting with radio waves to send communication signals. By 1901, Marconi was sending messages by Morse code across the Atlantic Ocean with radio waves.

Sweet Sounds

Early radio could only send signals. Then, in 1903, the Canadian Reginald Fessenden worked out a way to modulate, or change, a constant radio wave. Now radio waves could carry sounds - including the human voice and even music. This breakthrough led to the rapid development of radio technology. By 1922, according to one account of the time, there were more than a million radio sets in the United States.

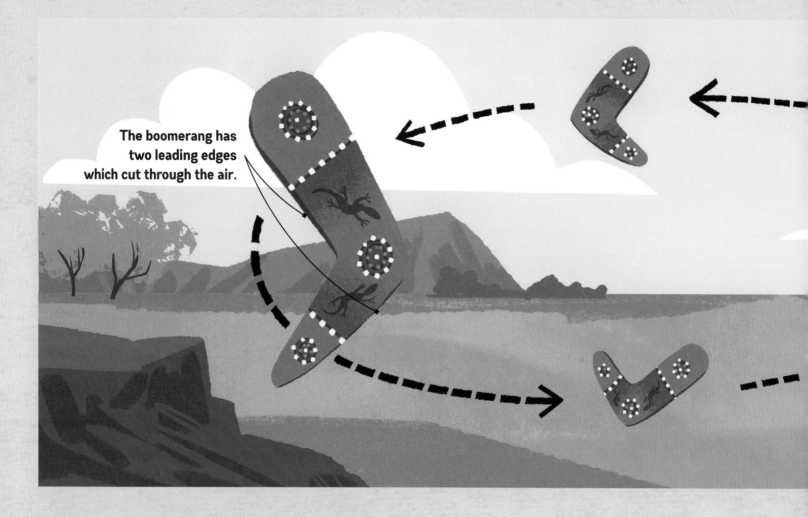

The boomerang has two leading edges which cut through the air.

Aerodynamics

If you throw something through the air, how far it flies depends on aerodynamics. Aerodynamics are the interaction between objects and the air moving around them. Things that are meant to be thrown, like balls, are shaped so the air slips over them easily. Things that aren't meant to be thrown, like a chair, are more bumpy. If you launched a chair into the air, the air would slow it down quite quickly, and it wouldn't go far.

Early peoples realized that sticks and stones were better for throwing than... er... less aerodynamic objects. But one culture went even further. About 30,000 years ago, a cave artist in Australia depicted hunters chasing animals such as kangaroos with special throwing sticks. Aboriginal Australians called these sticks 'boomerangs'.

It's Not Just a Stick!

Boomerangs are thin, nearly flat pieces of wood which were used mainly to hunt animals or as flying weapons. They spin through the air, flying straight and fast, because of their makers' understanding of aerodynamics. The key is the boomerang's shape. Its bottom is flat but the top is curved. As the boomerang flies, the air above it has to travel further over the curve than the air passing straight underneath. That creates lower air pressure above the boomerang, causing it to lift. Hey presto: a flying machine.

The boomerang spins as it flies.

Incoming!

A returning boomerang comes back to its thrower. It is shaped like a shallow V. When it is thrown and the lift comes into effect, the two arms spin around their axis, creating speed differences between the leading and trailing arms. This makes the boomerang come back – unless anything gets in the way, such as a stray emu.

It was millennia after Aboriginal peoples had been using boomerangs that Europeans such as Galileo Galilei began to investigate aerodynamics – and their research was inspired in part by studying another type of weapon: cannonballs.

+ Meet the Scientist · George Cayley (1773-1854)

At the end of the 1700s the English engineer George Cayley identified four forces that act on all flying objects: weight, lift, drag and thrust. Cayley was determined to build an aircraft, and his understanding of aerodynamics underlies the history of human flight. In 1804 he built a model glider and, nearly 50 years later, the first successful full-scale glider.

Building Blocks of Life

Biology

You are alive, and that is different from being not alive.
But what actually is life, and how are humans linked to the
plants and animals that share our world? For a long time,
people believed that the world had always been the same.
However, when scientists started investigating fossils
left by ancient life forms and studying variations in living
creatures, they discovered something very different.
There was a long history of change in living things.
Scientists also discovered the chemical principles that
explained the changes, from how humans are different from
other primates to why you might look like your brother
or sister, if you have one.

Cells

Cells are the building blocks of all living things. There are about 37.2 trillion cells in the human body, so you might think they would be difficult to miss – but they're far too small to see with the naked eye. They weren't discovered until the microscope was invented in the mid-1600s.

The first person to see cells was Robert Hooke, an Englishman who used his new microscope to examine a range of objects. In 1665 he published drawings of what he saw, including the first close-up of a fly's eye (terrifying!). Among his other subjects was a piece of cork. Hooke saw that the wood was made up of regular shapes that fitted together like a honeycomb. The shapes reminded him of the cells in which monks lived in a monastery, so he called them 'cells'.

Cell Science

Hooke had seen the walls of dead cells, but a decade later the Dutchman Antonie van Leeuwenhoek described living cells. Leeuwenhoek was a draper who had built a microscope to check the quality of the cloth he was buying. When Leeuwenhoek examined a form of water algae called spirogyra, he saw that each living cell had a central part, or 'nucleus', surrounded by other structures.

We now know that the nucleus and the other structures, called organelles, produce material and energy for making new cells, which is how the body reproduces, grows and repairs itself. New cells are only created when an older cell divides. The organelles carry hereditary information in every cell (see pages 32-33).

Cells, Cells – and Cells

Although the cells that made up plants were clear through a microscope, those in animals and humans were harder to see. Scientists continued to argue that animals were made from a different type of particle, called a globule.

That changed in 1838, when two German scientists, Theodor Schwann and Matthias Schleiden, went for coffee. Schwann was studying cells in animals and Schleiden was studying cells in plants. As they chatted, they began to realize that in fact they were describing the same thing. The cell was the building block of all living things.

Cell Copycats

The history of what is now called cell theory is full of themes that often crop up in stories of discovery: accusations of plagiarism, overlooked contributions and eagerness to take all the credit. Schwann and Schleiden did not acknowledge the work of another scientist, Rudolf Virchow. But Virchow himself was later accused of copying the work of Robert Remak to claim that all cells arise from pre-existing cells.

Theodor Schwann and Matthias Schleiden

Antonie van Leeuwenhoek

Spirogyra

Robert Hooke

Hooke's microscope

Heredity

When a blue flower breeds with another blue flower, the new flower they create is usually blue. This is the result of heredity, which is the passing of characteristics from parents to their offspring. The same process happens in plants and animals – including humans: characteristics pass from parents to their children. But in the mid-1800s, no one knew how.

Pea Power

In the 1860s, a Czech monk named Gregor Mendel grew more than 10,000 pea plants in the garden of his monastery. By studying characteristics such as height, flower colour and seed shape, he worked out that parent plants pass information to the next generation by chemical units, later called genes.

Humans have many genes, which determine different characteristics, such as eye colour. At reproduction, one gene of each type from each parent is combined. Different genes lead to variation between people in different ways, but in the simplest situation, if both genes are for brown eyes, the offspring's eyes are likely to be brown. If both genes are for blue eyes, the offspring's eyes are likely to be blue; if there is one gene of each, then one characteristic is dominant (in this case, brownness).

had been shown to directly affect physical characteristics – but Stevens did not receive full recognition for her discovery during her lifetime.

+ Meet the Scientist · Barbara McClintock (1902-1992)

Twenty-two years after Stevens's discovery, American scientist Barbara McClintock received a PhD in biology. She studied maize (corn) and mapped which parts of the chromosome influenced which characteristics of the plant. McClintock explained how chromosomes could switch genetic information 'off' and 'on' and move position. There was so much opposition to her studies that she stopped publishing her findings, but years later McClintock was recognized, and in 1983 she won the Nobel Prize for medicine.

No one took much notice of Mendel's work, but it was later rediscovered and became the basis of what in 1905 was named genetics. As understanding of heredity improved, scientists learned that genes were carried on structures in cells called chromosomes.

Sex Cells

The American Nettie Stevens was studying cells in 1905 when she noticed that male mealworm sperm had a pair of large and small chromosomes. Sperm with both large and small types led to male offspring, while females resulted from sperm with two large copies. She concluded that sex was decided by what are now known as the X and Y chromosomes. It was the first time chromosomes

Evolution

The answer to the question 'Who discovered evolution?' seems simple: it was Charles Darwin, one of history's most famous scientists. He worked out how species change over time by a process he called natural selection. But does Darwin deserve all the credit?

In natural selection, individuals with more useful characteristics for survival tend to have more successful offspring than others. These successful characteristics are preserved and multiply from generation to generation, so a species changes over time: this is evolution.

In 1859 Darwin published a book called *On the Origin of Species*, inspired by his studies of plants and animals while on a five-year voyage around the world. He noticed how species were adapted to their environments.

However, Darwin was not alone in his studies. In France, for example, the naturalist Jean-Baptiste Lamarck observed that parents passed on adaptations to their offspring and Georges Cuvier suggested that animals seemed to belong in related families. And in fact, Islamic scholars had put forward ideas of evolution 900 years earlier.

Rival Theory

Charles Darwin's idea, natural selection, explained the means by which species changed. But just as he was getting ready to publish his findings, he received a letter from British naturalist Alfred Russel Wallace.

The letter contained a precise outline of the very theory Darwin had just worked out.

When Darwin and Wallace's ideas were presented in London on 1 July 1858, you might have expected fireworks. After all, evolution contradicted the biblical story of the Creation. In fact, they made virtually no impact at all.

Noisy Debate

That soon changed with the publication of Darwin's book a year later, and his name became forever linked with evolution. Is this fair? Probably. Unlike Wallace's, Darwin's theory was hugely detailed and backed up with evidence. Darwin also worked extremely hard for it to gain widespread acceptance. Plus Darwin coined the phrase 'natural selection'. So on balance, he certainly deserves a huge amount of credit, if not quite all of it.

✛ Meet the Scientist · Alfred Russel Wallace (1823-1913)

Born in Wales, Alfred Russel Wallace became a teacher but later travelled to the Amazon to collect animals and plants. Wallace's collection of specimens was lost when his ship sank, but he survived and headed to the Malay archipelago in Asia, where he continued his studies. While sick with a fever, Wallace suddenly came to the same understanding as Darwin about how evolution happened – so he sat down to write him a letter.

DNA

After the discovery of heredity (see pages 32-33), scientists tried to learn how hereditary messages were passed from parents to their offspring. They learned that inside the nucleus of a cell, genes (which can be copied and passed on to the next generation) are carried on chromosomes. Chromosomes are tiny threads made up of protein and another molecule, deoxyribonucleic acid, or DNA for short – and DNA is the key to understanding heredity.

Putting the Evidence Together

Scientists had long known of the existence of DNA, but working out its structure was one of the most famous scientific discoveries of the 20th century. The Swiss chemist Friedrich Miescher had first identified DNA in the late 1860s, but no one had had the tools to work out what made up the molecule until the early 1950s, when two scientists, James Watson and Francis Crick, came up with better ways to understand the structure of proteins and other large molecules. It made them world famous – but they didn't do it alone: their discovery was only made possible because of the achievements of other scientists.

Explaining with X-Rays

The British scientist Rosalind Franklin was a pioneer of a technique called X-ray diffraction. She believed it could reveal key clues about materials such as protein, by using crystals of that material to break up, or 'diffract', an X-ray. Before Franklin began her work, very little was known about DNA, but she worked out its density and that it must have a spiral structure of some sort.

Discovering the Double Helix

Franklin's findings were to prove invaluable for Watson and Crick's discovery. They had imagined DNA as a triple helix – a spiral made up of three parallel strands. But Franklin took an X-ray image of DNA, called Photo 51, that made them think again. They came up with a model of a double helix, which was like a spiralling ladder with long sides joined by rungs.

Watson commented, 'When we saw the answer, we had to pinch ourselves. We realized it was probably true because it was so pretty'.

+ Meet the Scientist · Rosalind Franklin (1920-1958)

Rosalind Franklin is best known for her contribution to our knowledge about DNA, but she had many other achievements. Her research into the structure of coal led to it being used as a filter in gas masks during World War II, which saved lives. She also studied the structure of viruses, including the polio virus, and her research led to the development of a vaccine for the disease.

Photosynthesis

If you've got six weeks to start learning about photosynthesis, try this. Put some soil in a pot and weigh it. Then plant a seed – any seed – and leave it to grow. The soil and the plant now weigh more, so where did the extra weight come from? (If you haven't got six weeks, just read this.)

In the early 1600s, a Flemish man named Jan Baptista van Helmont did that very experiment. He figured out that the extra weight – his plants – could only come from the water he added to the pot. Close, but not quite. Water was only part of the story. There was also a chemical process occurring.

Injured Air

Late the following century, the Englishman Joseph Priestley showed that air contained different gases. In an experiment, he burned a candle under a glass dome with a mouse inside. In his own words he said that the candle 'injured' the air by using up some part of it until the candle went out and the mouse died. But when Priestley added a plant to the dome, the candle continued to burn – and the mouse stayed alive. (Luckily!) Whatever part of the air the mouse was breathing must be being released by the plant. At the time, however, no one knew what the gas was or how it was released.

Converting Oxygen

The Dutch scientist Jan Ingenhousz tried the same experiment, and he observed tiny bubbles coming from the plant's leaves during the day that stopped at night. That suggested that something about daylight was involved in releasing the gas.

The next step came when a Swiss pastor named Jean Senebier identified the gas being released as oxygen. He suggested that the leaves were taking in carbon dioxide and converting it to oxygen in their cells. It was left to a German surgeon, Julius Robert Von Mayer, to recognize the overall process of photosynthesis. This is when plants convert energy from sunlight into chemical energy.

We now know that a green pigment called chlorophyll in plants' leaves absorbs energy from sunlight. This energy, combined with water and carbon dioxide taken in by the leaf, produces sugar and other substances the plant needs to survive. Oxygen is a waste product of this process, and it is released from the plant into the air.

This conversion process goes on continuously, even at night. It was discovered in 1950 by the U.S. scientist Melvin Calvin and his colleagues, and it is sometimes called the Calvin Cycle.

Bring me Sunshine

Photosynthesis is the basis of nearly all life on Earth, because most living things depend on the energy of the Sun (there are some deep-sea creatures that can live without it). The energy made in plants from sunlight is transferred to whatever animals eat the plants, which are then eaten by other animals and so on. Meanwhile, all plants, from enormous trees in great forests like the Amazon to a herb in a window box, are part of the process of removing carbon dioxide from the atmosphere and replacing it with oxygen.

Classification of Organisms

The first attempts to group animals and plants based on their resemblances were made in ancient Greece by Aristotle and others. A pupil of Aristotle named Theophrastus, for example, classified plants into herbs, shrubs and trees in around 300 BCE.

As Europeans began to explore the world after the 1400s, they found the new plants they discovered confusing. How could they be named in a way that related them to European plants, or to each other?

Setting Up Species

The 17th-century naturalist John Ray classified plants he saw in Europe into species, based on their appearance and other characteristics. Ray's breakthrough was to see the importance of species, which he defined as a set of individuals who through reproduction give rise to new individuals similar to themselves. So, apples were a species, as were cows and bulls, as were peacocks and peahens – even though they looked completely different.

What's In a Name?

Ray's system laid the foundation for modern taxonomy – a way of classifying things. In 1735, the Swedish botanist Carl Linnaeus wrote a seven-page essay in which he grouped plants by their methods of reproduction. Linnaeus later began to use two-part names to describe the plant's genus and species. A genus is a group of related species – so dogs, wolves, coyotes and jackals belong to the genus *Canis*, but dogs are their own species, *Canis familiaris*.

Linnaeus tried to come up with memorable species names using a form of medieval Latin. In 1753 he gave two-part names to 5,900 species of plants. A few years later, he extended his scheme to animals. Although there have been many disputes over classification since, the Linnaean system remains one of the most remarkable scientific achievements.

Plant Hunters

From Sweden, Linnaeus sent out a generation of brave plant hunters to find and classify specimens around the world. Peter Kalm visited North America, Fredrik Hasselquist went to the Middle East and Pehr Osbeck travelled to China. Some of these explorers died from disease before they returned, but others went on to make huge contributions to growing botanical knowledge.

Carl Linnaeus

Kingdom
Phylum
Class
Order
Family
Genus
Species

The Linnaean classification system orders the natural world from kingdom to species.

Dinosaurs

In 1676, when the first dinosaur bone was found, it was mistaken for the thigh bone of a giant or an elephant. At the time, it seemed likely that a giant race of humans had existed. However the actual explanation was that a whole class of animals had existed – but no longer did.

It was only in 1842 that British palaeontologist Richard Owen started to put the clues together. He was an expert in animal anatomy who studied the fossils of three prehistoric animals: *Megalosaurus, Iguanodon* and *Hylaeosaurus*. Owen noticed that their skeletons were different to existing reptiles, and he suggested that the animals

were carnivorous, herbivorous and armoured members of a previously unknown family that he named Dinosauria, from the Greek meaning 'terrible lizard'.

Moving Picture

Owen suggested that the dinosaurs were large reptiles up to nine metres long that resembled four-legged animals such elephants or rhinoceros. It was soon clear he was wrong, however. New fossils revealed that some dinosaurs stood on two legs and were fast runners.

Other scientists began to doubt that the name dinosaur was useful at all. For nearly a century, it was rarely used. Then, in the 1970s, experts realized that all the dinosaurs did indeed seem to be related, so calling them all 'dinosaurs' was useful. They also realized that dinosaurs' closest living relatives were not lizards but birds.

Crater Disaster

At the same time, scientists began to wonder why the dinosaurs had died out. In 1980, Luis Alvarez and his son, Walter, suggested that a huge asteroid struck Earth about 65 million years ago. Debris choked the atmosphere and 75 per cent of species died – including most of the dinosaurs. The Alvarez theory was confirmed when a huge impact crater was identified at Chicxulub in Mexico in 1990.

+ Meet the Scientist · Mary Anning (1799-1847)

Richard Owen hunted dinosaurs on the Jurassic Coast of southern England, where the cliffs held many fossils. His guide was a local woman named Mary Anning, who from 1811 made a name as one of the country's leading fossil hunters. Mary found the first ichthyosaur skeleton and two nearly complete plesiosaur skeletons. She became famous but was never part of the mainstream scientific community, because she was a woman and because she followed a minority religion.

The First Humans

As soon as Charles Darwin suggested that humans had descended from apes, scientists started to wonder what stages lay in between. When did the first humans appear? And where? Was it in Africa, as Darwin himself suggested?

Early in the 1900s, fossil discoveries suggested that early humans had evolved in Asia, but the young Kenyan-born palaeontologist Louis Leakey was convinced humans had emerged in East Africa. He was so convinced, in fact, that his whole career was controversial – but his persistence paid off.

At Olduvai Gorge, a rocky ravine in Tanzania, Leakey and his wife Mary found traces of a series of early hominins (hominins include modern humans and our immediate ancestors). One, which was 1.75 million years old, had a strong ridge above the eyes – like gorillas have – and large teeth suitable for chewing tough plants. This was probably a species of *Australopithecus*, a genus that was closely related to and overlapped with the first humans.

Handy Tools
One of the Leakeys' most important discoveries was a later hominin without a brow ridge, and with

smaller teeth. Leakey guessed that this species had used tools to prepare meat for eating. The Leakeys found 'quarries' where individuals had shaped huge numbers of stones into tools for bashing and cutting. After some disagreement – which is very common when you're trying to piece together evolutionary history from ancient fossils – the hominin was recognized as one of our early ancestors. It was named *Homo habilis* ('handy man'), living between about 2.3 and 1.65 million years ago. It may have been the first hominin to use tools.

Later, Olduvai Gorge was home to *Homo erectus*, or 'upright man', who lived about 1.9 million years ago. According to modern theories, *Homo erectus* left Africa and spread across the world – but to be honest, that's still something of an educated guess...

+ Meet the Scientist · Mary Leakey (1913-1996)

As well as being a palaeontologist, Mary Leakey was a palaeoanthropologist – someone who studies the origins and development of early humans. She was better at excavating fossils than her husband – yet his skills in interpreting and publicising them meant that he often gets most of the credit. After her husband's death, she discovered footprints made by early hominins that had lived about 3.5 million years ago, preserved in volcanic ash. This remarkable discovery showed that people had walked upright earlier than previously thought.

Primate Behaviour

Have you ever watched a wildlife documentary on TV and thought, this is like watching my family? You were probably watching primates, the order of mammals that includes humans and our closest relatives: monkeys and apes. Two types of ape – chimpanzees and bonobos – share **99 per cent of their DNA with humans.**

From the time Charles Darwin came up with the theory of evolution, it was pretty clear just by looking at them that humans, apes and monkeys were related. Louis Leakey, who spent his lifetime looking for early human fossils in East Africa (see pages 44-45), was fascinated by the relationship between humans and primates. In 1960, Leakey and his young secretary, Jane Goodall, decided to find out more about early humans, and Goodall went to live with chimpanzees.

Join Our Troop

Goodall spent 15 years studying a troop of chimpanzees in Tanzania. Instead of observing them from a distance, she gave the chimps names and got so involved that they treated her like a member of the troop. She soon saw two things that completely changed experts' view of chimpanzees.

First, Goodall watched a chimp using a piece of grass to pull termites from a mound to eat. Previously, it had often been thought that humans were the only animals to use tools. Second, she watched the troop hunt, kill and eat a small colobus monkey. Chimpanzees were not peace-loving vegetarians!

The Little Monkeys!

The chimpanzee hunt may have mirrored how early humans worked together to hunt meat. Goodall also came to recognize that chimpanzees have individual personalities and express their emotions through sounds and gestures, and can interact with each other in complex ways – again, like humans. Such ideas were very unusual for the time – but suggested that Leakey was right about the similarities between humans and the great apes.

Gang of Three

Goodall wasn't the only researcher encouraged by Leakey to study primates. The American Dian Fossey was so determined to study gorillas that she taught herself Swahili before living in the field in Rwanda from 1966 until her death in 1985. In 1971, meanwhile, Leakey helped the Canadian-Lithuanian Biruté Galdikas establish a centre in Borneo to study orangutans. The three researchers were called the 'Trimates' because they studied primates.

Staying Healthy

Medicine

People today live longer, healthier lives than in the past. Until about 1800, the average life expectancy in Europe was about 30 to 40 years; today, it is more than 75 years. Of course, this reflects things like better food and improved living conditions, but it is also a result of a long process of discovering the causes of diseases and how they spread. These developments mean that we now understand just how important sanitation is. We have also learned how the body fights disease. This helps us understand how medicines work – some of which are ancient – and how to make more effective cures.

Blood Circulation

When William Harvey was born in Kent in 1578, anatomy was still dominated by the teachings of Galen, a Greek living in the Roman Empire in the 2nd and 3rd centuries. From his early insights looking after wounded gladiators, Galen had gone on to dissect animals – even giraffes and an elephant – but never a human.

Galen believed that blood was created in the liver and passed to the right and left sides of the heart, where it was refined with 'vital spirits'. It carried these vital spirits through the arteries to the major organs, but was used up by the time it reached the outer parts of the body.

Making Adjustments

Galen's book on anatomy was still an undisputed authority over a thousand years after he wrote it – despite his mistaken assumptions that human and animal anatomy matched. Around 1540 Flemish anatomist Andreas Vesalius began correcting Galen's ideas after human dissection became more common – though he still couldn't work out how the heart functioned.

Enter William Harvey, who studied medicine at Cambridge University before travelling to Padua,

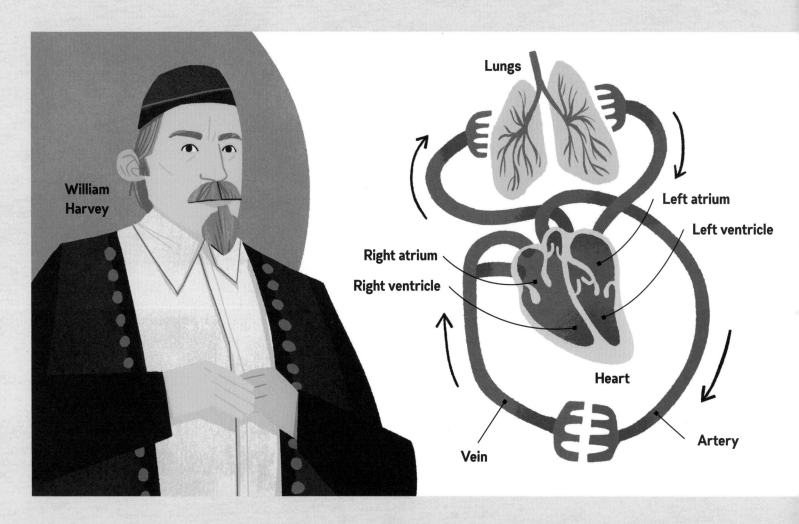

William Harvey

Lungs

Left atrium

Left ventricle

Right atrium

Right ventricle

Heart

Vein

Artery

Italy. There he observed dissections carried out by his teacher, Hieronymus Fabricius ab Aquapendente, who noticed that the veins had small valves that ensured that blood could only flow in one direction.

Life Machine

By dissecting living animals, Harvey worked out that blood flows from the right of the heart to the lungs, then back to the left side of the heart, from where it passes into the arteries. The heart acts like a pump to squeeze blood into the arteries – but the one-way valves suggested that the blood returned to the heart by the veins. Then it was pumped to the lungs to fill up with oxygen again before circulating around the body again. For the first time, Harvey had suggested that there was nothing mysterious about the heart.

It was a pump made from muscle – in which case, perhaps the human body was not much more than an interesting machine.

❓ What Would YOU Do?

Discovering how the human body worked was based mainly on dissection – in other words, cutting open dead bodies, often those of executed criminals. From the 1500s, anatomy students could watch as they were cut up in lecture theatres. Anatomists became so eager to get bodies to cut up that some governments had to pass laws to prevent people stealing dead bodies from graves. Do you think people should be allowed to cut up bodies to learn about anatomy? If not, how else might anatomical pioneers have been able to learn?

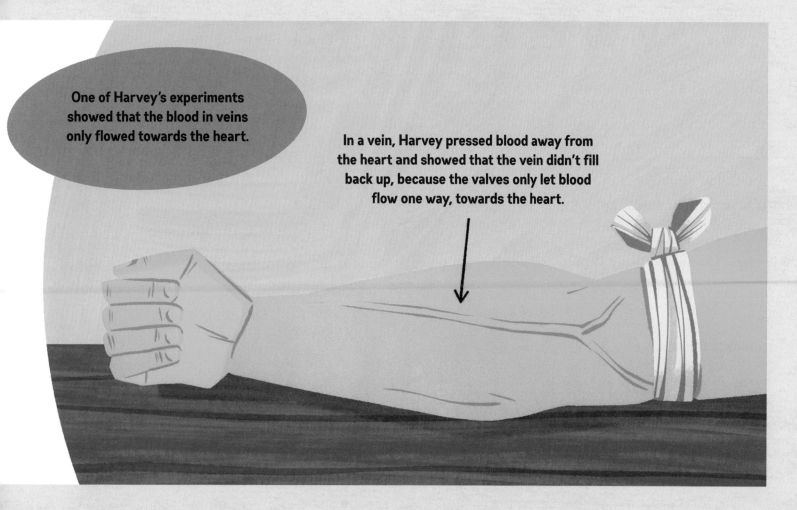

One of Harvey's experiments showed that the blood in veins only flowed towards the heart.

In a vein, Harvey pressed blood away from the heart and showed that the vein didn't fill back up, because the valves only let blood flow one way, towards the heart.

Germ Theory

The first person to suggest that some diseases are caused by microscopic bacteria and fungi – germs to you and me – may have been the Islamic writer Ibn Sīnā in the 11th century. Of course, he could not have described them as microscopic, as the microscope was not invented until 1590. There was no way to actually see anything as small as bacteria.

Other scientists later came up with similar theories, including the Italian physician Girolamo Fracastoro in 1546, in his book *On Contagion and Contagious Diseases*. It was not until over a century later that the Dutch scientist and keen user of the microscope, Antonie van Leeuwenhoek, used his new device to study bacteria from the inside of his mouth. Even then, no one thought that these bacteria were anything to do with germs and disease. Most people still believed that disease was spread by a 'miasma', or an invisible cloud in the air.

Germ Hunting

It took another 160 years for someone to come up with a comprehensive theory for how germs might spread disease. That was the German scientist Friedrich Gustav Jacob Henle in 1840. His theory was further refined by one of his students, Robert Koch, who devised a way to stain bacteria to make them easier to study under a microscope. That allowed a new type of scientist – called bacteriologists – to start hunting for specific bacteria that cause certain diseases, including typhoid, tuberculosis (discovered by Koch himself) and endemic dysentery.

French Pioneer

Another pioneer of germ theory was the French chemist Louis Pasteur, who became interested in microscopic organisms when he was asked to study vinegar that had gone off. He concluded that microscopic 'rods' in yeast in the liquid were living organisms carried in the air that spoiled the vinegar. Pasteur came up with a way to prevent microbes spoiling liquids such as vinegar and milk by heating and cooling them. In honour of Pasteur, this process was named 'pasteurisation'.

Pasteur also discovered a method to vaccinate people against rabies, even though the germs that cause the potentially fatal disease were too small to be seen by microscopes of the time. He created a weakened form of the disease that could be injected into patients to build immunity.

+ Meet the Scientist · Louis Pasteur (1822-1895)

One of Pasteur's breakthroughs was to disprove the theory of spontaneous generation. This idea had argued that tiny animals, such as germs, were created spontaneously from the air. It was only in the 1860s that Pasteur performed a series of experiments to show that microbes could only arise from other microbes.

Antonie van Leeuwenhoek

Girolamo Fracastoro

Ibn Sīnā

Robert Koch

Louis Pasteur

Vitamin C

Imagine you were asked to sail the world. Great! Now imagine that there was a 50/50 chance that your gums would rot, your skin would bleed and you might die. Would you still make the trip? That was the prospect facing sailors in the 1600s and 1700s thanks to a disease called scurvy.

Scurvy struck on long voyages, when sailors had no fresh food and lacked Vitamin C. Early Chinese sailors carried ginger to prevent the disease, and later peoples in India and North America showed Europeans how to combat its effects by eating citrus fruit or even boiled pine needles. These aids were usually forgotten or ignored by Europeans, however.

Oranges and Lemons

In 1747, the Scottish doctor James Lind was serving on a naval ship when the crew got scurvy. By treating patients in different ways – in what was one of the world's earliest clinical trials – Lind showed that oranges and lemons could cure scurvy (cider helped, too). But he still didn't know why. Like his contemporaries, he believed scurvy was caused by rotting food and unhealthy living conditions.

However, when the Navy issued daily lemon juice to sailors travelling to India, no one got scurvy. The Navy started giving lemon juice to all its crews. Even so, some people still believed keeping fit was a better defence against scurvy than what we now know is the Vitamin C in citrus fruits and other foods.

Vital Vitamins

Later in the 1800s, scientists began testing what was in foods. In 1912 a Polish biochemist named Casimir Funk called nutrients in foods 'vitamines', from the words vital and amines, which are a type of chemical. When it was discovered later that not all the substances were amines, the name was changed to vitamins.

If people lack certain vitamins it can cause disease. Beriberi, for example, which often occurs where diets are mainly white rice, affects the nerves and heart. It is caused by a lack of vitamin B1. Today, we know 13 vitamins, named after letters: A, B (eight types), C, D, E and K.

+ Meet the Scientist · Dorothy Hodgkin (1910-1994)

Vitamin B12 was discovered in 1948. Its structure was analysed by the British chemist Dorothy Hodgkin. She was a pioneer of using X-rays to create images of crystals of biomolecules. For her work on B12, she became only the third female chemist to win a Noble Prize, in 1964. (Four men also won Nobel prizes for studying Vitamin B12.)

Vaccination

During the Covid-19 pandemic, scientists raced to create a vaccine against this new disease that swept across the world. But vaccines are nothing new – they've been around for centuries.

Around 1,000 years ago, the Chinese noticed that people who survived a sometimes fatal disease called smallpox never got it again. Sufferers of smallpox are covered in blisters or 'pox'. In around 1000 CE, a Chinese monk made a powder from the scabs on smallpox blisters. A healthy person would breathe this powder in through their nose, which would provide immunity against (stop them getting) the disease. It sounds disgusting – but it worked, and it's called inoculation. The process was widely practised in Asia.

A Pox on You!

Some people who were inoculated did still catch smallpox and die, so a better treatment was needed. In 1796, an English doctor, Edward Jenner, noticed that milkmaids who suffered from a mild disease named cowpox did not catch smallpox. Jenner took pus from a cowpox blister and scratched the arm of a boy so he could put it into his skin. The boy got mild cowpox, but when Jenner injected him – deliberately! – with smallpox, he did not get the disease. Jenner carried out many experiments to show the vaccine was safe, and within 50 years, thanks to the vaccine, cases of smallpox had dropped dramatically.

Death to Disease

During the 1800s, scientists came up with vaccines against serious diseases, such as rabies, and in 1952, a vaccine against polio was developed by the U.S. doctor Jonas Salk. More than 450 million doses were distributed across the United States between 1955 and 1959, and cases of polio dropped dramatically. In 1980 the World Health Organization declared that smallpox had been eradicated from the whole world.

Some people are nervous of vaccines because they don't really understand how they work. Modern vaccines are made from non-harmful parts of bacteria and viruses that cause disease. When the body recognizes these intruders, the blood produces killer cells that target them and prevent them from increasing inside the body. That means the body has increased resistance to the real disease.

Turkish Delight

In the early 1700s, Lady Mary Wortley Montagu, the wife of a British diplomat living in Constantinople, in what is now Turkey, saw that inoculation was widespread there. Her brother had died of smallpox, and she herself had contracted it in 1715, but had recovered. Lady Montagu inoculated her children and was also responsible for introducing the technique to Britain and Europe, where it became popular among the rich.

Hygiene

If you go to a modern hospital, count yourself lucky: everything there is set up to stop disease spreading. But even 150 years ago, hospitals could be so unhealthy that the conditions made some people sicker and even killed them.

The fact that good hygiene promotes good health might seem obvious, but it wasn't discovered until the mid-1800s. Even before Louis Pasteur and Robert Koch confirmed that germs spread disease (see page 52), some people had started to promote good hygiene. In 1847 the Austrian doctor Ignaz Semmelweis recommended that doctors wash their hands before delivering babies, to prevent infection.

Cleaning Up

During the Crimean War (1853–56), British nurse Florence Nightingale took a group of nurses to run a British army hospital in Turkey. In the hospital, more soldiers were dying of disease than of their wounds. Nightingale soon found out why: the hospital was filthy and short of supplies.

Nightingale encouraged the less badly injured patients to scrub the wards. She also made sure her nurses washed bedclothes – and the patients – regularly, and opened the windows to allow fresh air to circulate. The death rate dropped by two-thirds. Nightingale went on to collect statistics linking hygiene to good health, laying the foundations for modern nursing.

On the Front Lines

In 1849, Elizabeth Blackwell was the first woman to graduate from medical school in the United States. She worked around the world, studying how poor living conditions affected disease. During the American Civil War (1861–65), Blackwell helped set up the Women's Central Association of Relief to coordinate care for the wounded. Along with Dorothea Dix, the Superintendent of Army Nurses, she campaigned to improve sanitation in military hospitals, ensuring that other medical professionals came to recognize that hygiene was key to patients' recovery.

❓ What Would YOU Do?

During the American Civil War, diseases such as dysentery killed at least twice as many soldiers as the fighting. The hygiene of army camps was appalling, with open sewage ditches and millions of lice and mosquitoes that spread disease. What hygiene rules would you use to maintain health in a large camp where soldiers lived close together?

+ Meet the Pioneer · Mary Seacole (1805–1881)

The Jamaican businesswoman Mary Seacole was also a pioneer in sanitation during the Crimean War. She cared for soldiers at the battlefront, becoming known as 'Mother Seacole'.

Antibiotics

Antibiotics save millions of lives by preventing infections caused by bacteria, but the first widely available antibiotic, penicillin, was discovered by accident by Scottish scientist Alexander Fleming.

People had noticed thousands of years earlier that some biological substances (that's the bio in anti*biotics*) could prevent infection. The ancient Egyptians, for example, pressed mouldy bread against wounds. This never really took off as a treatment, however, and even in the 1800s infectious diseases, such as pneumonia and diarrhoea, still killed millions of people around the world.

Staining Cells

In the 1870s, as a student, the German physician Paul Ehrlich had been staining cells with chemical dyes when he noticed that different dyes coloured different bacteria. If there were different types of bacteria, he realized, it should be possible to use chemicals to kill them without damaging other parts of the body. In 1909, Ehrlich and his Japanese colleague, Sahachiro Hata, discovered a chemical that killed the bacteria that caused the disease syphilis.

That's Careless!

This is where Alexander Fleming, who supposedly wasn't very good at tidying away his things, comes in. In 1928 he forgot to put a lid on a petri dish where he was growing bacteria. He noticed that a fungus had grown on the dish – and killed the bacteria. Fleming isolated the active part of the fungus and called it *Penicillium notatum*.

Mass Manufacture

A decade later, a team of scientists at Oxford University started figuring out how to mass-manufacture penicillin as an antibiotic. Their work became even more urgent after World War II broke out the following year. By 1944, when Allied troops invaded Nazi-occupied Europe, they took supplies of penicillin that saved the lives of thousands of wounded soldiers.

Disease Destroyer

The name 'antibiotic' was first used by Selman Waksman, a Ukrainian-born American microbiologist. Waksman isolated more than 15 different antibiotics by studying microbes in soil, including two that became widely used to treat infections resistant to penicillin. Streptomycin, which was found by Waksman's students Albert Schatz and Elizabeth Bugie, was the first antibiotic that could treat the severe disease tuberculosis.

Elizabeth Bugie

Painkillers

Do you ever take a tablet or liquid medicine to get rid of a headache? You might think of painkillers – officially known as analgesics – as being a modern invention. But drugs were being used by people as long ago as the Babylonians and ancient Greeks, and probably even earlier. And some of them were very like the drugs we still use today.

Medical books from ancient Assyria – now Turkey – mention the opium poppy plant and the drug harvested from its sap. The Greeks named the sap opion, which led to its modern name: opium. Opium and the drugs which can be made from it – called opiates – prevent the brain from sensing pain signals from the body.

Plant Pain Relief

The Greeks discovered the medicinal benefits of other plants, such as the willow tree. Women chewed willow bark or drank a tea made from its leaves during childbirth to give them some pain relief. Later, in the Americas, the Aztec and other South American peoples used the bark of the cinchona tree to cure malaria, a disease spread by mosquitoes. These natural cures were passed down from generation to generation.

Exploring Chemicals

In the first half of the 1800s, European scientists began to investigate what chemicals in natural substances actually had a medical effect. In 1820, French scientists learned that quinine in the bark of cinchona was what cured malaria. And in 1828 a German pharmacologist called Johann Andreas Buchner found out that the painkilling substance in willow bark was salicylic acid. Scientists learned to isolate quinine and salicylic acid from their sources. They used them as drugs.

A German chemist named Felix Hoffmann learned how to create salicylic acid in the laboratory. In 1899, the new drug, named Aspirin, went on the market. It was the first drug that was sold all around the world.

❓ What Would YOU Do?

Making medicines raises all sorts of issues. Say you discovered a substance that acted as a miracle painkiller – but that made some people so addicted that it ruined their lives. Would you still produce and sell it? That scenario is actually happening now. Some opiates produce a drowsy state that some people find extremely addictive. They may be given the drugs by their doctor for a specific problem, but once they start taking opiates, they find it extremely hard to stop, and this has a very bad effect on their health. These opiates kill more than 40,000 people every year in the United States.

Super Sciences

Maths & Chemistry

From Plato in ancient Greece and Galileo Galilei in Renaissance Italy to modern cosmologists, scientists have believed for centuries that the universe can be best understood through maths. Their belief has been underlined by studies of the elements – the basic chemicals of matter. It turns out that the structure of atoms that make up elements is dictated by maths, including the numbers of subatomic particles they contain, the electrical charge they carry and even how quickly they spin. An increased understanding of these particles that we cannot even see has opened the way to the so-called atomic age.

Zero

Discovering nothing sounds a bit like not discovering anything, but in actual fact, the discovery of zero was really something. It changed mathematics – and enabled the invention of your computer and smartphone.

Zero seems like a simple idea, but it's more complicated than it sounds. It doesn't really exist in nature: for example, say you have no apples. There are lots of times you don't have any apples. But you also don't have lots of other things. Why would you even notice not having any apples, unless you particularly wanted an apple? And why would you need to write down that you had zero apples? Nothing is the absence of anything, so that's just what it is: nothing. Confused? Well, yes. So was everyone else for thousands of years!

Holding a Place
Nothingness is easier to pin down in mathematics than in nature. In maths, zero has two uses. One is to do with writing out large numbers. Counting systems like the one we use today (technically called the Hindu-Arabic number system) use the position of a digit in a number to indicate value. So, writing 103 shows that there is one hundred, and three ones. The zero indicates that the tens column is empty. It's just a placeholder. In ancient Mesopotamia in about 1600 BCE, people used a double-wedge shape in the same way.

Showing Nothing
The second use of zero is to signify an absence, or a lack, of quantity. This originated in India, probably in the mid-400s. Indian merchants used black dots to indicate zero in their accounts. Another Indian, Brahmagupta, defined zero and how it operated in maths in 628 CE.

Nothing Spreads
The idea of zero reached Europe in the 1100s via the Islamic world, where it had been further developed by the Persian scholar Muḥammad ibn Mūsā al-Khwārizmī. By now the sign for zero was the same empty circle we use today: 'O'. As the Italian mathematician Fibonacci recognized, O and the digits from 1 to 9 enabled people to write all numbers easily. This was far simpler than earlier number systems, so it made doing calculations much easier. For the first time, maths was no longer for specialist mathematicians but for *everyone*.

+ Meet the Scientist · Acharya Pingala (3rd/2nd century BCE)
Pingala was an Indian scholar from the second or third century BCE, who came up with the idea of a binary system: a system with just two values. Pingala called the values heavy and light, but they also expressed presence and 'nothingness' – a Buddhist idea called sunyata. Today, all computer programs rely on a binary system that is usually written using 1 and O – so all our smart devices depend on zero!

The Mesopotamians wrote on clay tablets in a script called 'cuneiform'.

Muḥammad ibn Mūsā al-Khwārizmī

Fibonacci

Brahmagupta

Computer Language

Do you speak binary? That's how computers are programmed, with two symbols (bi means two) that are usually written as 0 and 1. The first person to suggest that it was possible to communicate using binary was the Indian scholar Pingala over 2,000 years ago, and the idea still fascinated people such as the German Gottfried Wilhelm Leibniz in the 1600s.

Binary couldn't become a computer language until there was a computer. Step forward the English engineer Charles Babbage, who, in the 1830s, designed an 'Analytical Engine' to carry out mathematical calculations through a system of mechanical gears. Think big – a modern day replica of this machine isn't the size of a calculator, it's the size of a room!

The English mathematician Ada Lovelace saw Babbage's idea and suggested that it would be possible to use punch cards with holes that were either open or closed – a binary code – to instruct the machine to carry out different calculations. Similar punch cards were used in looms for weaving, and she said, "The Analytical Engine weaves algebraic patterns, just as the Jacquard loom weaves flowers." Lovelace is credited as creating the first ever computer program.

It's Logic

Another English mathematician, meanwhile, was fascinated by whether he could reduce logic (a way of mathematical thinking) to a series of simple calculations. In 1854, George Boole came up with what he called an 'algebra of logic' that was based on two values: true and false. The symbols he used for true and false? 1 and 0, of course.

Boole wasn't thinking about computers, but in 1940, about 75 years after his death, the American mathematician Claude Shannon realized that the chains of on/off switches in early computers corresponded exactly with Boolean logic. Shannon saw that circuits could be used to do any kind of mathematical calculation based on two simple instructions: 0 and 1. And today, Boolean logic is used in many programming languages.

+ Meet the Scientist · Grace Hopper (1906-1992)

In the 1940s and 1950s, the U.S. naval mathematician Grace Hopper was frustrated with hard-to-understand computer languages. She came up with a new programming language that used English words, making it far easier to write programs, and invented a 'linker' which turned the English terms into a code that could be read by the first electronic computers.

Algebra

People had been doing maths with numbers for centuries before they started doing maths with letters: in other words, algebra. Algebra has fascinated some of the smartest maths brains in history since it offers a whole new way to present and solve problems... even if they don't have any numbers!

Algebra is essentially a way to solve mathematical problems by using symbols and equations to work out missing values. An equation is a mathematical sentence. Algebra uses letters like x and y instead of numbers, where the number isn't known. So, in the equation $12 - x = 4$, you can work out that x must equal 8, because $12 - 8 = 4$.

X + Y = Algebra

People started using algebra in ancient Babylon, which is now part of Iraq, nearly 4,000 years ago. The Babylonians solved equations by working out the squares and cubes of numbers, and recorded their calculations by pressing a reed stylus into soft clay.

Other peoples also developed their own forms of algebra, including the Egyptians and the ancient Greeks, as well as the Indians and Chinese. But the person who came up with something close to modern algebra lived in the same part of the world the Babylonians had. Muḥammad ibn Mūsā al-Khwārizmī – he's often known as al-Khwārizmī – was born in Persia but spent most of his life in Baghdad, now in Iraq. In around 820 CE, al-Khwārizmī wrote *Al-Kitāb al-mukhtaṣar fī ḥisāb al-jabr wa'l-muqābala – The Compendious Book on Calculation by Completion and Balancing*. The term 'al-jabr' led to the English name algebra.

Equations Equal Fun

Al-Khwārizmī showed how to try to reduce the terms on either side of an equation – for instance, by removing terms that occurred in both places – and then balancing what remained. He discussed solving equations as mathematical problems in their own right – a tradition that has shaped modern Western mathematics.

Algebra remains its own field of study, separate from the use of maths to solve practical problems, and it has attracted some of the most famous thinkers in history, including the 17th-century French philosopher René Descartes. He first came up with using x to indicate the first unknown term in any equation.

The House of Wisdom

Al-Khwārizmī worked at the House of Wisdom – the nickname of an academy in Baghdad that attracted outstanding scholars from throughout the Abbasid Empire. Al-Kindī, for example, translated Greek works into Arabic while Abū 'Uthman al-Jāḥiz from Iraq, was one of the first people to suggest that animals such as dogs and wolves had a common ancestor. Other scholars made notable advances in astronomy and the study of 'optics', or sight, as well as inventing many new mechanical devices.

Air   Water

Fire   Earth

Nature of Air

These days, there's a lot that scientists know about gases. They know there's more gas in the universe than anything else: just two gases, hydrogen and helium, make up 98 per cent of everything that exists. They also know that our bodies take in oxygen from the air and eliminate carbon dioxide out into the air. But it wasn't until the 1600s that anyone realized that the air was actually a mixture of different gases.

The ancient Greeks knew that air is important for life. They counted it as one of the four ingredients called 'elements' that made up everything around them. These were air, water, fire and earth. In the fifth century BCE, a Greek named Empedocles argued that different combinations of these substances accounted for all matter.

This theory still dominated science in the Middle Ages. However, although people believed that air was an element, they could see that it came in different forms, such as fogs and mists.

Into the Void

In the early 1600s, a Flemish chemist named Jan Baptista van Helmont noticed that when charcoal was burnt, the amount of ash that was left behind afterwards was far less than the original amount of charcoal. He thought that part of the charcoal had been released as an invisible substance during burning, and he was correct: we know now that carbon dioxide is released when charcoal is burnt.

Jan Baptista
van Helmont

Daniel
Rutherford

Van Helmont named such invisible substances 'gases', based on the Greek word *chaos*, meaning empty space or void.

Noxious Air

For the first time, scientists had an idea that air was made up of different gases. In the 1700s, scientists began to analyse what those gases might be by burning various chemicals and trapping the gases they produced. At the time, combustion (burning materials) was thought to release a substance called 'phlogiston' that was contained within everything.

In 1722, the Scottish physician Daniel Rutherford removed carbon dioxide from air and was left with what he called 'phlogisticated air', or noxious air: nothing could burn in it or breathe it. This turned out to be the gas nitrogen, which makes up 78 per cent of the air around us.

More Gases

The discovery of oxygen and hydrogen soon followed. Oxygen makes up 21 per cent of the air around us – and the remaining one per cent is made up of lots of different gases, including hydrogen, carbon dioxide and what are called 'noble gases'.

This group of gases was discovered in the late 1890s. The new noble gases – argon, helium, neon, krypton, xenon and radon – all shared similar qualities and were highly stable, which means that they don't react easily with other elements. For that reason, they were named the 'noble gases' and given a whole new group in the periodic table (see pages 74-75). 'Argon' even means 'the lazy gas' because it is so unreactive.

Periodic Table

Most scientists agree that 92 chemical elements occur naturally – but some are so rare that only a few grams exist. There are currently 118 known elements, but this could change if new ones are found. If they are, they should fit into a table devised more than 130 years ago.

That table was created by the Russian Dmitri Mendeleev, who studied chemistry in St. Petersburg and later became a professor. While preparing to write the first Russian textbook on inorganic chemistry (chemistry that doesn't involve carbon), Mendeleev decided to organize the known elements into a logical order.

Put Your Cards on the Table

Other people had tried ordering elements previously, but not all chemists agreed on the characteristics that could be ordered – or even that atoms existed. Mendeleev wrote out each element on a card, with its atomic weight and a description of its characteristics. Then he started to lay out the cards in columns in order of atomic mass. Each time the character of the elements changed, he started a new column.

Mendeleev ended up with a grid with seven horizontal rows, or 'periods', and 17 columns, or 'groups' (plus two long sequences which are usually printed separately). Each group, we now know, has the same number of electrons in the outer shell of each atom, so they react in similar ways chemically. The Group 1 elements, for example, which are called alkali metals, all react strongly with cold water: sodium, for instance, fizzes and whizzes around on the water's surface. The noble gases of Group 18 are odourless, colourless and slow to react.

Changing Qualities

Since its first creation, the periodic table has been refined. Mendeleev himself revised it only two years later, in 1871, moving 17 elements. When no element fitted a slot, Mendeleev left it empty, predicting that new elements would be found to fit – and they usually were. He gave three of these elements the names 'eka-boron', 'eka-aluminum', and 'eka-silicon'. These have since been discovered and are called scandium, gallium and germanium.

Women and Elements

Elements have been named after various things, but a few celebrate the contribution of female chemists. Element 109, meitnerium, was named in honour of Austrian-Swedish physicist Lise Meitner, who discovered protactinium in 1917. Polonium is named after Poland, the homeland of the chemist Marie Curie, rhenium for the birthplace on the Rhine of one of its discoverers, Ida Noddack, and francium after the homeland of the French chemist Marguerite Perey.

MEITNERIUM

Mt

109

Radioactivity

Radiation often gets a bad name because it can be harmful – but it's also one of the most important types of electromagnetic energy in the universe. It's an invisible form of energy that can penetrate various materials, which is why it sometimes causes disease within living things. But there are also many harmless forms of radiation – including some given off by the bones in the human body!

Radiation was an accidental discovery. After German physicist Wilhelm Röntgen discovered X-rays in 1895, French physicist Henri Becquerel was investigating whether he could create X-rays from the Sun's energy. He planned to expose photographic plates containing uranium to sunlight – but it was too cloudy. Becquerel's plates emitted energy anyway, even without sunlight. The energy was radiating from the uranium.

Let's Get Rocking

Marie Curie, a Polish-born French physicist, soon began studying radiation with her husband, Pierre. They got hold of some rocks containing uranium, but when they extracted the uranium they found that the ore (material) left over was even more radioactive. They concluded it must contain different radioactive elements, and came up with the term 'radioactivity'. After four years – and a lot of ore – they assembled enough material to describe two new elements in 1898: polonium and radium.

Marie
Curie

Ernest
Rutherford

Particle Physics

More work on radiation was carried out in the 1910s by New-Zealand-born Ernest Rutherford, who also made breakthroughs in understanding the structure of atoms. He discovered that there are different types of radiation. Alpha particles are huge, they move slowly and they barely penetrate material. Beta particles are smaller and move faster, but can still be stopped quite easily. Gamma particles can penetrate large distances through materials, and they are highly dangerous to the human body.

✚ Meet the Scientists · The Curie family

The Curies were a remarkable scientific family. Between Marie, Pierre, their daughter Irène and son-in-law Frédéric, they won five Nobel prizes. Marie Curie was both the first woman ever to win the Nobel prize, and the first person to win it twice. She devoted much research to the practical medical uses of radiation.

Atomic Theory

The idea that everything in the universe is made from tiny particles began in ancient Greece. The word atom comes from Greek for 'indivisible' because an atom could not be split into smaller parts. It took until the late 1800s for scientists – yes, it took more than one – to confirm that atoms weren't so indivisible at all.

During the 18th century, Croatian mathematician and astronomer Roger Boscovich suggested that atoms were all identical and that the nature of a substance was decided by how far apart its atoms were. Then, in 1803, English chemist John Dalton concluded that gases were made up of tiny indestructible balls that could combine to form compounds, or 'molecules'. He wasn't quite right, but his theories were an important step forwards in understanding atoms.

Something Smaller?

The idea of an indestructible atom lasted until the 1830s, when the British scientist Michael Faraday performed an experiment which passed an electric current through water containing a dissolved chemical compound. He guessed that the current was pulling apart atoms that were held together by electrical forces, suggesting that atoms are actually made up of smaller, or 'subatomic', particles.

That idea was confirmed in 1897 by English physicist J. J. Thomson, when he discovered electrons – or, as he initially called them, corpuscles. Thomson suggested that atoms were like plum puddings, with these negatively charged electrons like plums held together by a positively charged 'dough'.

A New Model

In 1911, this theory was abandoned for a new model, put forward by New-Zealand-born British physicist Ernest Rutherford, who was actually Thomson's student. He suggested that an atom had a dense nucleus (centre), surrounded by moving electrons.

In turn, Rutherford's Danish colleague, Niels Bohr, then suggested that the orbits (movements) of the electrons were defined, circular orbits. The model was completed in 1932, when English physicist James Chadwick discovered neutrons, which, together with protons, form the nucleus of an atom.

+ Meet the Scientist · Maria Goeppert Mayer (1906-1972)

Today, scientists think the nucleus of an atom is a tightly bound core of protons and neutrons, and that the surrounding electrons are like a cloud. The stability of the nucleus depends on the exact number of protons and neutrons it contains. This 'nuclear shell' model of the atom was proposed in the late 1940s by a number of scientists, including the German-born American Maria Goeppert Mayer. Mayer worked out that the so-called magic numbers that achieve greater stability are 2, 8, 20, 28, 50, 82 and 126.

Niels Bohr proposed that electrons move around at specific distances from the nucleus.

Ernest Rutherford suggested that an atom had a dense central nucleus.

J. J. Thomson discovered electrons.

James Chadwick proved that protons were inside the nucleus of every atom.

Nuclear Fission

Every atom has a nucleus (centre) containing protons and neutrons. Most atoms, when left alone, don't do much. But atoms can release enough energy to power huge bombs. And if you're reading this by electric light, the electricity might have been generated by a power station that also relies on the energy locked inside atoms.

Nuclear reactions to create energy – for bombs or power stations – rely on the most famous equation of all time: $E = mc^2$. Einstein's equation says that energy (E) is equal to the mass (m) multiplied by the speed of light squared (c^2). A small amount of mass can release a huge amount of energy. When atoms are forced to collide with each other, their mass is converted into energy.

A Snowy Walk

Before the 1930s, scientists were busy working out the structure of the atom (see pages 78-79). Once they had done this, they tried to find out more about atomic nuclei (their centres). One way of doing this was to bombard uranium with neutrons. And this is what Austrian physicist Lise Meitner had been doing with her colleague, Otto Hahn. They produced something called isotopes of barium.

This was interesting because, according to scientific knowledge about nuclei at the time, it wasn't actually possible.

In 1938, Meitner spent Christmas with her nephew and fellow physicist Otto Frisch. They went on a walk through the snow and stopped at a tree stump to discuss the problem. They came up an idea that would explain what had happened in Meitner and Hahn's experiments: a nucleus was like a drop of water. When it was hit by a neutron, it might stretch and grow thinner in the middle – until it eventually broke into two smaller nuclei. It would also release a huge amount of energy.

Chain Reaction

When Frisch wrote about the discovery, he named the process 'fission', which was the term biologists used when cells divided. Fission could occur again and again in a chain reaction, which would keep on going. The tiniest particles in the universe could be used to create a huge amount of power.

❓ What Would YOU Do?

One use of fission was in the creation of the atomic bomb, an immensely powerful bomb that ended up killing hundreds of thousands of people. Meitner was appalled that her discovery helped to create the atom bomb – yet the bomb helped defeat the Japanese in World War II (1939–1945). What if you discovered something brilliant (really, you might!) but people wanted to use it in a way you disagreed with, like Meitner? How would that make you feel? Do you think discoverers should have any control over what happens to their discoveries?

81

5.

Third Planet from the Sun

Earth

Our ancient ancestors lived in close harmony with the planet, both on land, where landscapes range from deserts and swamps to mountains and canyons, and at sea, where water circulates through the oceans in a huge system that influences the globe's climate. By closely observing the world, scientists have discovered not only many of the hidden structures that shape it, but also the harm humans can do to it. These discoveries led to the emergence of an environmental movement that will play an important role in shaping everyone's lives in the coming decades.

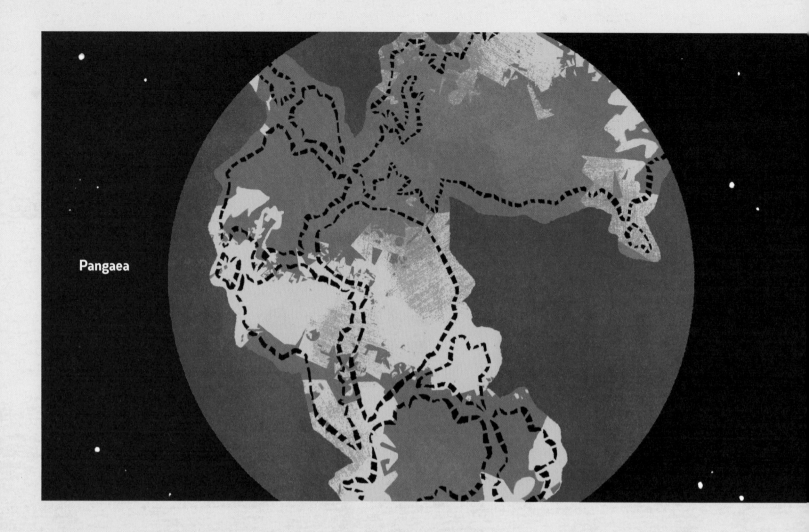

Pangaea

Continental Drift

Look at the map of the world on page 85. If you glance at the Americas and Africa, what's the first thing that strikes you? They look as if they fit together, right? In which case, why are they 2,500 kilometres apart?

People first noticed the similarities between the continents at the end of the 1500s, during what is sometimes called the European 'Age of Discovery', although the idea of places being 'discovered' would have surprised the people who already lived there. A Dutch mapmaker named Abraham Ortelius suggested that South America and Africa had been ripped apart by earthquakes and volcanoes.

How Did They Get There?

Three hundred years later, geologists studying rock formations were even more convinced that in fact all of Earth's continents had once been joined. But no one knew how they had moved.

In 1912, a German geologist named Alfred Wegener suggested what he called continental drift. Wegener said all the continents once belonged to a single landmass, which he called Pangaea, but had drifted apart. For 30 years, scientists rejected his theory – mainly because no one could work out what made continents move. Then in the second half of the 20th century, a new theory appeared: plate tectonics.

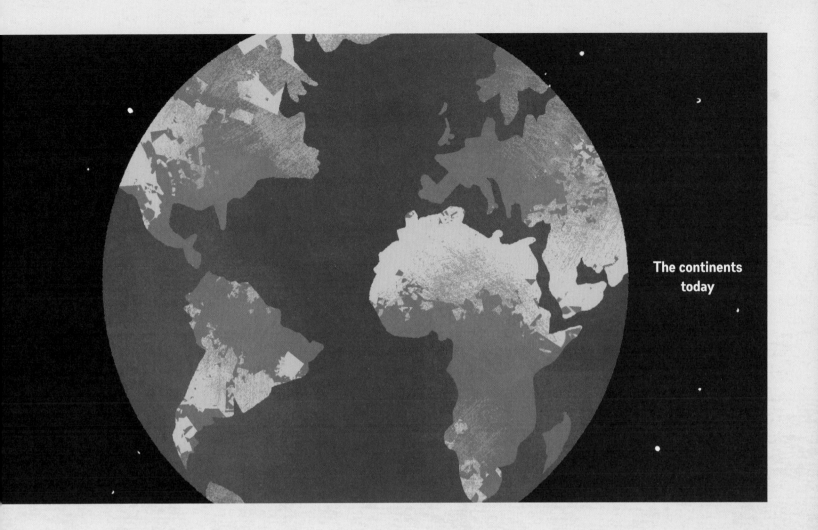

The continents today

Plate Tectonics

This theory confirmed that Wegener was right: the continents move. The continents are huge plates floating on a layer of semi-solid rock called the mantle. The mantle is in constant motion as hot material from near Earth's core rises while cooler rock sinks. Earth's plates – there are seven large ones and several smaller ones – move. The edges where the plates meet are often marked by volcanoes and earthquakes. Where plates push into one another, they can force up Earth's crust into huge mountain ranges, such as the Himalayas.

✛ Meet the Scientist · Marie Tharp (1920-2006)

In the 1950s, U.S. oceanographer Marie Tharp solved a mystery of plate tectonics. While making a map of the bed of the Atlantic Ocean, she discovered a deep rift valley running north to south through its heart. There, new rock from the mantle rises up and joins the plates on either side. This pushes apart Europe and Africa on one side, from the Americas on the other, at the rate of about 2.5 centimetres a year.

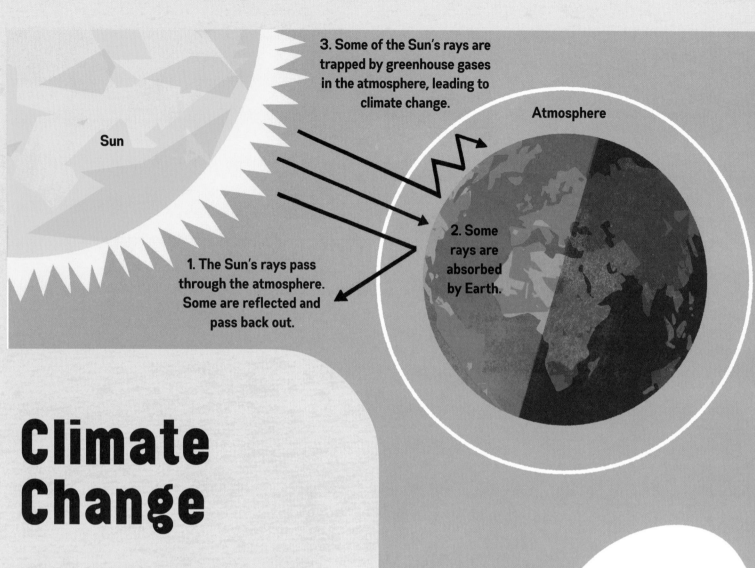

3. Some of the Sun's rays are trapped by greenhouse gases in the atmosphere, leading to climate change.

Sun

Atmosphere

1. The Sun's rays pass through the atmosphere. Some are reflected and pass back out.

2. Some rays are absorbed by Earth.

Climate Change

Today, everyone knows how harmful it will be if the global temperature rises because of climate change. In September 2019, millions of people in 185 countries marched to protest against climate change. You might have been one of them. Or you might have taken part in a Fridays for Future school strike. But the first discoverers of climate change thought its effects might be positive...

In the 19th century, the Swedish scientist Svante Arrhenius suggested that basic chemistry showed that increased carbon dioxide (CO_2) in Earth's atmosphere would lead to a rise in global temperatures. Setting out to explain why Earth went through warmer and colder phases, Arrenhuis argued that increased CO_2 in the

atmosphere, caused by burning fossil fuels, would cause a 'greenhouse effect' by trapping the Sun's energy. Arrenhuis incorrectly thought this might actually be positive, saying people might live 'under a milder sky and in less barren surroundings'.

Caused by Humans

In the middle of the 20th century, Canadian-born engineer Guy Stewart Callendar agreed with Arrhenius. He compiled data to show clearly that Earth was getting warmer, and he argued that human activity (which causes an increase in CO_2 in the atmosphere) was playing a large part in this temperature rise.

Modern Crisis

People such as Arrenhuis and Callendar laid the groundwork for climate change to become a major issue in the 1970s. Between 1945 and 1975, global temperatures fell, but then they began to rise again and the question became more urgent. Scientists began to warn that human activity could cause the atmosphere to start an inexorable rise in global temperature. The rate of human emission of CO_2 into the atmosphere was growing at an ever-increasing rate.

By the end of the 1980s, thanks to the work of experts such as U.S. professor James Hansen, global scientists largely agreed that human activity caused climate change – and that urgent measures were needed to prevent long-term harm to Earth. That was the start of the modern climate change movement – and led directly to today's school strikes to try to save the planet.

+ Meet the Scientist · Eunice Newton Foote (1819-1888)

Eunice Newton Foote was one of the first people to suggest that CO_2 would heat the atmosphere. She tested CO_2 and other gases to see which trapped the most heat, concluding that: 'An atmosphere of that gas [CO_2] would give to our Earth a high temperature.' Her findings were published but didn't find an audience until they were rediscovered by chance in 2010.

Conservation

Humans have always interacted with and changed the environment around them, for example by burning forests to clear land for farming. Many early peoples had deep respect for their surroundings, as do modern peoples such as Native Americans, but humans are also capable of causing great harm to the world around us.

With the rise of industry and its dirty, polluting machinery in the late 1700s, environmental damage started to take place on a large scale. Many individuals were horrified at this. In the United States in the 1800s, people began to argue that remarkable landscapes were worth protecting. In 1872 the first national park was created at Yellowstone in Wyoming to preserve the landscape for everyone to enjoy. This marked the start of the modern conservation movement.

A Birdless Future

During the first half of the 1900s, damage to the environment grew worse as the world's growing population needed more homes, food and energy. The American naturalist Rachel Carson became aware of the damage caused by pesticides used by farmers to protect their crops from insects.

In 1962, Carson's book, *Silent Spring*, imagined a world in which no songbirds survived, having been killed by a pesticide named DDT. Without birds, she warned, ecosystems would collapse.

Carson was opposed by agricultural and chemical companies, who accused her of trying to reverse scientific progress, but she did change public opinion. Eventually, in 1972, the U.S. government placed severe restrictions on DDT use. Fourteen years later it was banned in the U.K.

❓ What Would YOU Do?

Carson took on powerful opponents in the agricultural and chemical industries. If you faced similar opposition, how could you go about making your case? Would you stage protests and marches, or post on social media? What do you think the most effective way to get powerful corporations to listen would be?

✛ Meet the Scientist · Marjory Stoneman Douglas (1890-1998)

American conservationist Marjory Stoneman Douglas campaigned to protect a unique wetland region: the Everglades in Florida. In 1969 she founded 'Friends of the Everglades' to protect the area. Aged 79, she fought to reduce pollution from U.S. Army drainage works and sugar industries in the region.

Ocean Currents

As soon as people began sailing away from the land, they realized that the waters of the ocean are in motion. Huge currents move in a continuous pattern as a result of the winds, the spinning of the Earth, water temperature, ocean depth and the saltiness, or 'salinity' of the water.

The early people who understood this best were the navigators of the Pacific Ocean. More than 50,000 years ago, people from Southeast Asia sailed to Australia. Southeast Asia and Australia were closer together then, because sea levels were lower, and land bridges would have connected places that are now divided by ocean. However, these people must have sailed some parts of the journey, for example between Bali and Lombok, which would have required voyages of at least 200 kilometres. By about 1500 BCE, people of the Lapita culture were spread across the Pacific islands as far as Samoa in the east and New Caledonia in the south.

Sailing Away

The settlers did not sail to new islands by accident, for example by being swept off course by the winds. The winds mainly blew from the east, so the settlers were deliberately steering *into* them. They used double-hulled canoes with sails and outriggers (second hulls for balance) to keep them stable, allowing them to carry people and animals to their new homes.

The settlers navigated by the stars, but their travel also required a deep understanding of the currents and winds. The Pacific has four main currents, so maintaining a course is difficult, especially into the wind.

I Recognize this Place!

As well as following the stars, navigators also observed the movement of birds and the swell of the sea waves – which changed shape closer to land or above an ocean current – the colour and shape of the clouds and even the smell of the water. Navigators sometimes lay in the bottom of the boat so they could feel its motion more easily. They also used sticks and pebbles to make 'charts' of the stars in the sky, the islands and the currents of the sea. They passed on information about navigation in stories, called aruruwow, that were handed down orally from generation to generation.

Before 1000 CE, the Pacific islanders had reached Hawaii, in the heart of the ocean, over 3,500 kilometres from its nearest neighbour.

Humboldt Current

In 1802, German naturalist Alexander von Humboldt measured the temperature of the Pacific Ocean and identified a current of cool water running up the coast of South America. The water only measured about 16°C, even though tropical seas are usually far warmer, because winds were drawing up water from the deep ocean to the surface. This created a nutrient-rich ecosystem for many fish, birds and sea mammals. Around one-fifth of all the fish caught in the world comes from what is now called the Humboldt Current.

Beyond Our Planet

Space & Time

In science fiction movies, space is often called the final frontier. With better telescopes that allow us to see deeper into the distant universe and instruments that allow us to analyse the elements present in stars, cosmologists are learning more about the structure of space and our role within it. Many of these discoveries have taken place within the last century: only 100 years ago, astronomers were not even certain that other galaxies existed. It seems very likely that space is still hiding many discoveries of the future.

Planetary Motion

From the ancient Greeks to early Christians, ideas of the heavens above Earth were based on the idea that it was a perfect realm – unlike Earth – in which planets moved in circles. And they moved around Earth, which was clearly the most important part of the universe. Because, well... just because.

The problem was that this didn't match what astronomers could see in the night sky. The planets changed distance from Earth, their speed varied and at times they appeared to travel backwards. Early astronomers such as the 2nd-century CE Egyptian–Roman Claudius Ptolemy tried to explain these differences by suggesting planets moved within a complex series of circles within circles.

Circles Are Square!

Ptolemy's idea lasted over 1,000 years, despite scientists such as the Arab astronomer Ibn al-Haytham – known in the West as Alhazen – pointing out that it was clearly wrong. In the 1300s, another Arab, Ibn al-Shatir, suggested a new, simpler model of the universe that was based on what he could actually see at night. Like Ptolemy he placed Earth at the centre of the universe and assumed the planets moved in circles, but he removed many of the complexities of earlier systems.

Around 150 years later, the Polish astronomer Nicolaus Copernicus published a description of the universe in which the planets orbited the Sun, not Earth. Apart from that detail – okay, it's a pretty big detail – Copernicus's ideas matched those of Ibn al-Shatir.

Using the Observations

Copernicus had placed the Sun at the centre of the universe, but he still struggled to explain how the planets actually moved. That mystery was finally solved after a Danish noble named Tycho Brahe set up his own observatory, where he made highly accurate observations of the five planets known at the time. Brahe's results were analysed by the German astronomer Johannes Kepler, who finally saw the truth. The planets did not travel in a perfect circle, but in an elliptical trajectory (oval path) that made them speed up and slow down relative to one another as they moved closer to or further from the Sun.

Human Computers

In the 1960s, the National Aeronautics and Space Administration (NASA) employed a group of African American women as 'computers' or mathematicians to work out problems involved in space flight. One of these scientists, Katharine Johnson, calculated the precise journey that would need to be followed by the Friendship 7 spacecraft, which carried John Glenn into space, and made him the first American to orbit Earth.

Claudius Ptolemy

Ibn al-Shatir

Johannes Kepler

Nicolaus Copernicus

Galaxies

In the 1700s, a French astronomer named Charles Messier used a telescope to locate comets – balls of dust and ice that pull or push trails of dust as they orbit the Sun. Messier was very good at finding comets – he discovered 13 – but he grew irritated when he found objects that seemed fuzzy, like comets, but that turned out to be fixed in the sky.

Messier began to catalogue these smudges, or 'nebulae'. Some people suggested these 'island universes' were collections of stars outside Earth's local galaxy, the Milky Way. However, because most people believed the Milky Way was the whole universe, they argued the nebulae must be clouds of gas inside it.

Magic Telescope

That was still the view in the 1920s, when the U.S. astronomer Edwin Hubble used a brand-new, powerful telescope to study a spiral-shaped smudge identified by Messier. Using stars called Cepheid variables, he calculated that this Andromeda Nebula was too far from Earth to be part of the Milky Way. It was about 2.5 million light years away.

Although his contemporaries mocked his ideas, Hubble insisted that Andromeda was a

Today, a lot of research into the distant universe is carried out by a telescope orbiting Earth in space. This Hubble Space Telescope is named for Edwin Hubble, the discoverer of galaxies.

+ Meet the Scientist · Henrietta Swan Leavitt (1868-1921)

Cepheid variables, the pulsing stars that enabled Hubble to measure the distance to the Andromeda Galaxy, were discovered by fellow American, Henrietta Swan Leavitt, in 1912. Working at the Harvard College Observatory, Leavitt catalogued variable stars from thousands of photographic plates, and worked out the relationship between their brightness and the speed of their pulse – known as their 'period'. This relationship, now known as Leavitt's law, allows the stars' distance from Earth to be measured.

different galaxy – and that the universe held far more galaxies than anyone had ever imagined. Hubble catalogued these galaxies for their shapes: elliptical, spiral and lenticular.

Big Space, Big Numbers

Hubble's discovery suddenly made space bigger. Much bigger. The latest estimate is that the universe contains 200 billion galaxies, although some astronomers say it is more like 10 *trillion*. The Milky Way contains about 100 billion stars, so that means the universe might contain 10 trillion x 100 billion stars. That's 1 followed by 24 zeros: 1,000,000,000,000,000,000,000,000!

Dark Matter

Earth's galaxy, the Milky Way, contains an estimated 100 to 400 billion stars, and the universe probably has more than 200 billion galaxies. All those stars, planets, moons, gas, dust, plants, people and more make up a lot of matter (stuff, basically). But the matter that scientists know about only makes up about five per cent of the total amount of matter in the universe: most of the universe's matter is unknown.

How do we know this? Well, by observing how the things we *can* see behave. Soon after Isaac Newton published his theory of gravity in 1687 (see pages 12-13), astronomers began to wonder if large, unseen objects might be diverting or blocking light from other sources. In the 1700s, the French scientist Pierre-Simon Laplace suggested there might be objects so massive that no light could escape from them (something very similar did turn out to exist: black holes). The next century brought the discovery of the planet Neptune in 1846. It hadn't previously been seen – but the effect of its gravity had, and scientists had predicted its existence.

Where's the Mass?
In 1933, the Swiss astronomer Fritz Zwicky studied a group of galaxies named the Coma Cluster. Zwicky calculated the mass of the galaxies and then figured out how much mass it would take to generate enough gravity to hold them together. The second figure was about 400 times more than his first total. He reasoned that something unknown must be holding the galaxies together. Because he couldn't see it, Zwicky called it 'dark matter'.

Galactic Puzzle
Dark matter, also known as the missing mass, existed as an idea for decades before its existence was actually proved.

How did this finally happen? Well, astronomers studying the range of electromagnetic signals given off by galaxies realized something: objects near the centre of galaxies and objects near the outside of galaxies rotate at the same speed. This is odd, because usually you would expect stars in the centre of a galaxy to rotate much quicker. They decided that something must be holding the outer stars in place, otherwise they would be flung into space. But whatever this thing was, it was not something that could be detected. It wasn't just a dark, slow or cold version of matter, therefore, but a completely different type of matter altogether.

Providing Evidence
One of the first astronomers to produce evidence of dark matter was the U.S. astronomer Vera Rubin. In the 1970s there were few female astronomers – at one observatory, Rubin cut out a female shape herself to stick on the door to create a ladies' toilet!

Rubin and her colleague W. Kent Ford studied the speeds at which galaxies rotate using a piece of kit Ford had built called an Original Image Tube Spectrograph, which could be attached to larger telescopes. Rubin provided the first physical evidence of dark matter, which she calculated outnumbered ordinary matter in galaxies by between five and ten times.

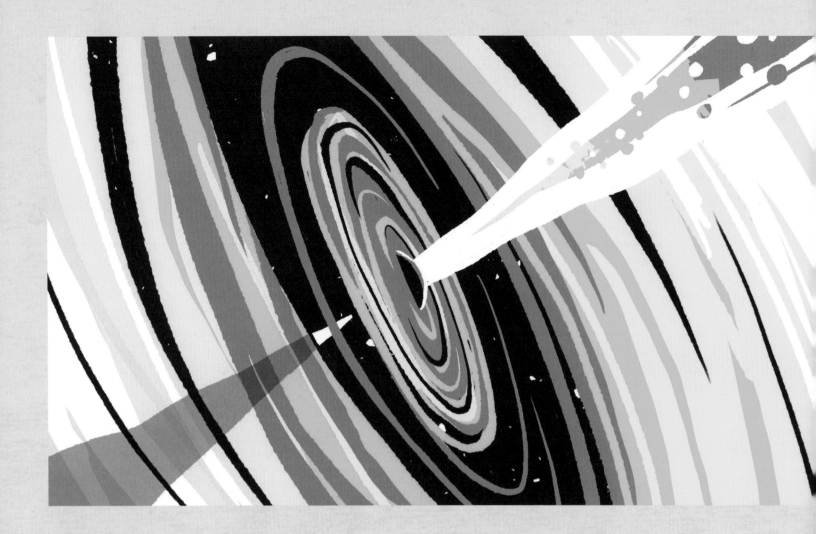

Black Holes

A black hole isn't really a hole. It's an object in space so massive that its gravity won't let light escape. It occurs when a giant star comes to the end of its life and begins to collapse in on itself, creating an 'event horizon' – a surface from which nothing escapes, not even light. Welcome to the world of relativity.

Our best guide to this idea is the German scientist who came up with it: Albert Einstein. His law of general relativity introduced the idea of spacetime, in which the gravity of huge objects warps both space and time, like heavy balls sinking in a rubber sheet. That's why time slows at the event horizon of a black hole and why no light can escape.

The idea of super-dense black holes in space was actually put forward by the German scientist Karl Schwarzschild in 1916. And he wasn't the first: in 1783, the English astronomer John Michell had tried to calculate the mass of stars by judging the speed of the light they emitted. The bigger the star, he suggested, the more its light would be slowed down by gravity. If a star was big enough, its gravity would stop any light escaping, making the star invisible to observers.

Not a bad guess, considering that Michell lacked powerful telescopes, calculators and computers. But his idea was so far ahead of its time that it didn't become popular until Schwarzschild solved Einstein's equations and put forward the idea of black holes.

Back to Black

Black holes remained theoretical until the 1960s, when the British astronomer Jocelyn Bell Burnell discovered pulsars – dense neutron stars created when supergiant stars collapse under the weight of their own gravity. That led to a new period of interest in the effect of gravity on huge stars – and in black holes, which were the ultimate result. Further research in the 1960s and 1970s taught scientists more about the properties of black holes – but still their presence was only assumed, not proven.

Today, we know that black holes occur at the heart of most galaxies. But what's inside – well, that's another question.

Cygnus X-1

Along with predicting the existence of black holes, John Michell also said the best way to identify them would be if a star were orbiting them. In 1972, Louise Webster and Paul Murdin in London and a Canadian student named Tom Bolton independently identified just such an object. It was an invisible source of intense X-rays that was orbiting a star about 6,000 light years from Earth. Named Cygnus X-1, the invisible object is now regarded as the first black hole ever to be identified.

Gravitational Waves

In 1915, Albert Einstein predicted that the gravity of all moving objects makes ripples in the fabric of space and time. These ripples are called gravitational waves. They are invisible but incredibly fast, travelling at the speed of light, and they spread out like the ripples in a pond when a stone is thrown in.

Einstein predicted them, but how could scientists prove these ripples actually existed? Often the events that cause them happen so far away that, by the time the gravitational waves reach Earth, they are very weak and hard to detect.

As Predicted

Ninety-nine years after Einstein predicted them, a team of researchers actually detected gravitational waves for the first time. They came from two black holes colliding in deep space, making a huge splash in spacetime. The collision actually happened 1.3 billion years ago, but it took that long for the waves to reach Earth.

In 2017, three American scientists – Rainer Weiss, Kip Thorne and Barry Barish – won the Nobel Prize for their groundbreaking work.

Super Smart Kit

In fact, we should also credit the piece of kit that made the detection of gravitational waves possible:

the Laser Interferometer Gravitational-Wave Observatory (LIGO). It's phenomenally smart. At two centres in the United States, one in Louisiana and another in Washington State, LIGO uses lasers to detect ripples in spacetime caused by passing gravitational waves.

LIGO Lasers

Both LIGO sites have two 4-kilometre-long tunnels at right angles to each other. This is called an interferometer. Gravitational waves stretch and squeeze space, and this stretching and squishing changes the lengths of the interferometer arms, affecting the lasers inside them and causing a flicker of light. If there are similar flickers at both LIGO sites, scientists know the patterns were caused by a gravity wave.

❓ What Would YOU Do?

In 1969, the American scientist Joseph Weber claimed to have detected the first gravitational waves using a special piece of equipment he had designed. But no one took him seriously because when other scientists built their own versions of his equipment to try to recreate his findings, they didn't detect anything. Unfortunately for Weber, a discovery that can't be repeated by anyone else can't be proved, and is pretty useless! What would you do if you thought you had discovered something but no one believed you?

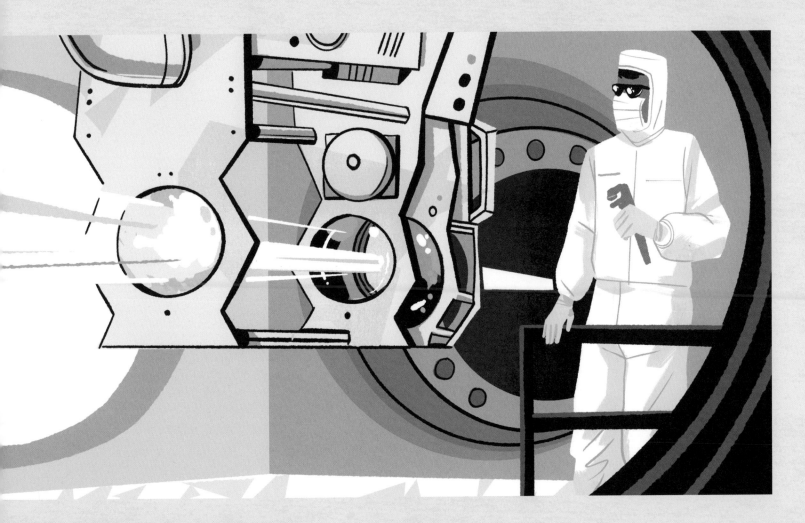

What's Next?

In this book, we've learned about important discoveries that have explained key facts about the world around us, what shapes it, and all the stuff in it. And, of course, there are far more discoveries that we *haven't* been able to fit into these pages.

There are still major discoveries to be made: some mysteries that scientists are actively trying to solve, and others that we can't even imagine yet.

For example, in space we are still looking for Earth-like planets outside our solar system and evidence of alien life. (Don't worry – this life is much more likely to be in the shape of microorganisms such as fungi rather than green creatures with two heads and laser guns.) And although cosmologists are pretty sure that the universe began with a Big Bang, they're still looking for clues about what happened *before* the Big Bang.

Closer to Home

Some discoveries waiting to be made concern our planet. We know more about the surface of the Moon than we do about the deepest parts of the oceans, which still have not been explored. And when it comes to humans, scientists still want to

discover why people age and whether there is any way to prevent it. We might also come up with ways to store our brains and thoughts in computers or other devices, though that would obviously raise some important questions about what a human actually is. It also reminds us that computers are highly powerful – so powerful, in fact, that we haven't figured out yet whether they will continue to help humanity or whether one day they might harm us.

Large and Small

There are discoveries left to be made at the very largest scale – perhaps by discovering whole parallel universes to ours – and at the very smallest. Physicists are searching for a subatomic particle called the axion, whose existence was first suggested in 1977 as a way to explain some of the basic forces at work in the universe – but which remains a suggestion rather than a fact.

More to Come

It's clear that there's lots still to be discovered. While you go through your own life discovering different things you didn't know, remember that the human race is going through a similar journey, working out why things happen (or don't). Although we have countless discoveries behind us, there are definitely many, many more to come in the future.

Timeline

1450s

1450 William Harvey describes how blood circulates around the body due to the action of the heart

1670s

1676 The first dinosaur fossils are discovered and thought to be a missing race of giant humans

1680s

1687 Isaac Newton publishes his laws of motion and the Universal Theory of Gravitation

1750s

1752 Benjamin Franklin flies a kite in a storm to show the electrical nature of lightning

1800s

1800 Alessandro Volta creates the first electric battery

c. 1801 Thomas Young demonstrates that light is a wave

1830s

1831 James Ross discovers the location of the magnetic North Pole

1840s

1842 Richard Owen identifies ancient fossils as belonging to a vanished class of animals he names 'dinosaurs'

1843 Ada Lovelace publishes the idea that a calculating machine could follow a series of instructions – the first computer program

1845 Julius Robert von Mayer suggests that photosynthesis converts light energy from the Sun into chemical energy

1665 Robert Hooke publishes drawings of cells that he has seen through a microscope

1666 Newton uses a prism to split light into colours

1660s

1747 Scottish surgeon James Lind notes the beneficial effects of citrus fruits against scurvy

1749 Émilie du Châtelet translates Newton's *Principia*, adding her own observations about the conservation of energy

1740s

1772 Daniel Rutherford isolates nitrogen from air

1774 Joseph Priestley discovers oxygen, which is named by Antoine Lavoisier a few years later

1770s

1820 Hans Christian Ørsted proves the existence of electromagnetism

1820 French scientists isolate quinine from a South American tree and use it to prevent and cure malaria

1822 Michael Faraday creates the first electric motor

1820s

1858 The ideas of Charles Darwin and Alfred Russel Wallace about evolution are presented in London

1850s

1735 Carl Linnaeus introduces a new system to classify plants based on how they reproduce

1730s

1860s

1860 Friedrich Gustav Jacob Henle describes the germ theory of the cause of disease

1864 James Clerk Maxwell deduces that light is a form of electromagnetic radiation

1865 Gregor Mendel presents the results of his investigations into pea plants, showing how units he calls 'factors' influence heredity

1865 James Clerk Maxwell publishes his laws of electromagnetism

1869 Dmitri Mendeleev publishes his periodic table of the elements

1900s

1901 Guglielmo Marconi transmits radio signals across the Atlantic Ocean

1903 Reginald Fessenden learns to modulate radio signals to allow broadcasting of the human voice

1910s

1911 Ernest Rutherford suggests that an atom has a dense nucleus surrounded by orbiting electrons

1912 Henrietta Swan Leavitt uses Cepheid variables as a way to calculate the distance of space objects from Earth

1912 Casimir Funk isolates beneficial substances in foods and names them 'vitamines'

1912 Alfred Wegener proposes the continental drift theory that Earth's continents have moved location

1915 Albert Einstein writes his General Theory of Relativity

1919 Ernest Rutherford discovers the proton

1940s

1940 Claude Shannon explains computer programs using Boolean algebra

1944 Penicillin is mass produced in time to help the Allies in the final year of World War II

1950s

1953 James Watson and Francis Crick publish their discovery of the double helix structure of DNA

1980s

1980 The World Health Organization announces the eradication of smallpox thanks to vaccination

---

1886 Heinrich Hertz sends and receives the first artificial radio waves

1880s

1895 Wilhelm Röntgen discovers X-rays

1896 Henri Becquerel discovers radioactivity

1897 Electrons are identified by J. J. Thomson

1898 Marie Curie discovers the elements radium and polonium

1899 The Bayer Company in Germany markets the first aspirin, isolated by the chemist Felix Hoffman

1890s

1928 Alexander Fleming accidentally discovers the antibiotic penicillin

1929 Edwin Hubble publishes research identifying Andromeda as another galaxy, making the universe infinitely larger than before

1920s

1932 James Chadwick discovers the neutron, which makes up an atomic nucleus together with protons

1933 Fritz Zwicky proposes the existence of missing material in the universe, which he calls 'dark matter'

1938 Otto Frisch and Lise Meitner work out the process by which nuclear fission occurs

1930s

1972 The first black hole, Cygnus X-1, is discovered simultaneously in Britain and Canada

1970s

1962 Rachel Carson reveals the dangers of pesticides in *Silent Spring*

1964 Louis Leakey announces his discovery in Tanzania of *Homo habilis*

1960s

2017 Astronomers win the Nobel Prize for Physics for detecting gravitational waves, whose existence was predicted at the start of the 1900s

2019 A Covid-19 pandemic starts to sweep the world, sparking the rapid development of vaccines, which are in use by the end of 2020

2010s

Glossary

aerodynamics – the study of the interaction between moving air and solid objects

algebra – a form of maths in which letters and symbols are used to represent numbers

anatomy – the study of the bodily structure of humans and other living organisms

antibiotics – medicines that prevent the growth of microorganisms such as bacteria

bacteria – a large group of single-celled organisms that can cause disease

binary – describes a system that uses only two numbers or ideas, such as 0 and 1

botanical – related to the study of plants

carbon dioxide – a colourless, odourless gas produced by burning substances or by humans breathing out that can contribute to global warming

cells – the microscopic particles that make up all living organisms, consisting of a nucleus and other material within a membrane

chain reaction – a chemical reaction in which the chemicals produced mean that the reaction continues to take place

chlorophyll – the green pigment in plants that absorbs sunlight for photosynthesis

chromosomes – threadlike structures in cells that carry genetic information

classification – arranging plants and animals into related groups

climate change – a change in Earth's climate patterns, particularly through human activity, such as burning fossil fuels

compound – a substance comprised of two or more elements

cosmologists – people who study the origins and evolution of the universe

dissection – the systematic cutting up of a dead body in order to understand its anatomy

ecosystems – groups of plants and animals that interact with one another and with their environment

electricity – a form of energy created by charged particles, such as electrons, that can either be stored in objects (static electricity) or move as a current

electrodes – poles through which electricity enters or leaves a substance such as liquid

electromagnetism – the phenomenon created by the interaction between electrical currents or fields and magnetic fields

elements – the basic substances of matter, which cannot be broken down by chemical means into other substances

energy – the ability to do work, or power to do work derived from physical or chemical sources

force – an influence that produces motion or stress in a physical object, or that makes a moving object change its motion

galaxy – a system of millions or billions of stars, with gas and dust

genes – units of heredity passed from parents to their offspring

geologists – people who study the materials that make up Earth

heredity – the biological processes by which parents pass characteristics to their offspring

isolate – to separate a pure form of something

isotopes – forms of elements that contain different numbers of neutrons in their nuclei

kinetic energy – energy a body has by being in motion

logic – an analytical way to think about a particular subject or problem

magnetism – attractive or repulsive forces between objects, caused by electrical charge

matter – physical substances that take up space and possess mass

microbes – microorganisms, particularly those that cause disease

microscope – a device for making tiny things visible

molecule – a group of atoms that is tightly joined together

natural philosopher – in the past, someone who studied nature and the physical universe

naturalist – someone who studies living plants and animals

neutron star – a very small, very dense star

orbit – the curved path of objects around larger objects, such as planets around a star

organs – structures in the body with specific purposes, such as the heart, lungs and brain

pesticides – artificial substances used to kill pests that harm crops

photons – particles that represent quanta, or 'packets', of light or electromagnetic radiation

physics – the branch of science that studies the nature and properties of matter and energy

potential energy – energy an object possesses because of its position relative to other objects, or to stress or electrical charge within itself

quanta – 'packets' of light or electromagnetic radiation

radioactivity – the emission of high-energy electromagnetic waves that can harm living organisms

relativity – the dependence of physical phenomena such as light, time and gravity on the relative position of the observer and the observed objects

reproduction – the way in which plants and animals produce offspring

species – a group of animals or plants in which individuals can reproduce to produce similar offspring

subatomic – related to the particles that make up an atom

telescope – an instrument that makes distant objects more visible

theory – an idea or system of ideas that explains something by using established facts

vaccination – inserting substances into the body to prevent infection by specific diseases

variable stars – stars whose brightness appears to alter

wavelength – the distance between two crests in a phenomenon such as electromagnetism, which travels as a wave

X-ray – a form of electromagnetic wave that can pass through materials through which light cannot

Find Out More

Discovery

+ The Science Museum in London, with many online objects and stories:
www.sciencemuseum.org.uk

+ A timeline of some of the most important scientific discoveries and inventions:
www.explainthatstuff.com/timeline.html

Making Things Move

+ A site devoted to Isaac Newton and his discoveries in the fields of gravity, optics, physics and mathematics:
www.sirisaacnewton.info

+ An exploration of electricity and its uses, with the story of its discovery and use for different applications:
www.explainthatstuff.com/electricity.html

Building Blocks of Life

+ A page from BBC Bitesize that answers the question 'What is evolution?':
www.bbc.co.uk/bitesize/topics/zvhhvcw/articles/z9qs4qt

+ A timeline of the major discoveries in heredity and genetics from the National Human Genome Research Institute:
www.genome.gov/Pages/Education/GeneticTimeline.pdf

Staying Healthy

+ Information about Florence Nightingale from the Florence Nightingale Museum in London:
www.florence-nightingale.co.uk/free-learning-resources/

+ The homepage of the museum set up in the home of Edward Jenner, who gave the first vaccination in 1796:
www.jennermuseum.com

+ A timeline of medical discoveries from Harvard Medical School:
https://hms.harvard.edu/about-hms/history-hms/timeline-discovery

Super Sciences

+ A BBC guide to how Dmitri Mendeleev created the first periodic table and how it changed chemistry:
www.bbc.co.uk/bitesize/guides/zxmmsrd/revision/1

+ An article from *Scientific American* magazine that explains the history of zero:
www.scientificamerican.com/article/what-is-the-origin-of-zer/

Third Planet from the Sun

+ A page from National Geographic with maps that show how the shape of the planet changed throughout history thanks to continental drift:
www.nationalgeographic.org/encyclopedia/continental-drift/

+ A NASA page explaining what climate change is and how we know it is happening:
climate.nasa.gov/evidence/

Beyond our Planet

+ An illustrated guide to galaxies from NASA:
www.spaceplace.nasa.gov/galaxy/en/

+ A National Geographic page about black holes:
www.kids.nationalgeographic.com/explore/space/black-holes/

+ The story of gravitational waves and how LIGO helped detect them for the first time:
www.spaceplace.nasa.gov/gravitational-waves/en/

Index